CHARLEMAGNE

WORLD LEADERS   **PAST & PRESENT**

CHARLEMAGNE

Susan Banfield

CHELSEA HOUSE PUBLISHERS
NEW YORK
PHILADELPHIA

SENIOR EDITOR: William P. Hansen
ASSOCIATE EDITORS: John Haney
            Richard Mandell
            Marian Taylor
EDITORIAL COORDINATOR: Karyn Gullen Browne
EDITORIAL STAFF: Pierre Hauser
            Perry Scott King
ART DIRECTOR: Susan Lusk
LAYOUT: Irene Friedman
ART ASSISTANTS: Ghila Krajzman
            Carol McDougall
            Tenaz Mehta
COVER DESIGN: Carol McDougall
PICTURE RESEARCH: Juliette Dickstein

   5   7   9   8   6

Library of Congress Cataloging in Publication Data

Banfield, Susan. CHARLEMAGNE

    (World leaders past & present)
    Bibliography: p.
    Includes index.
    1. Charlemagne, Emperor, 742–814—Juvenile Literature
2. France—History—To 987—Juvenile literature.
3. France—Kings and rulers—Biography—Juvenile
literature.   I. Title.   II. Series.
DC73.B34   1986   944′.01′0924   [B]   85-3760

ISBN 0-87754-592-8
    0-7910-0621-2 (pbk.)

Photos courtesy of AP/Wide World Photos, The Bettmann Archive, The
New York Public Library and Routledge & Kegan Paul Ltd.

The table on page 19 is reproduced from *The Coronation of Charlemagne* by Robert Folz, London, 1974, courtesy of Routledge and Kegan
Paul PLC

Contents

On Leadership, Arthur M. Schlesinger, jr. 7
1. In His Father's Footsteps 13
2. Young and Hot-Blooded King 21
3. Defeat and Despair 31
4. Years of Conquest 41
5. Settling in at Aachen 57
6. In Charge of Minds and Souls 67
7. The Road to Empire 79
8. Charles the Great 89
Further Reading 108
Chronology 109
Index 110

JOHN ADAMS
JOHN QUINCY ADAMS
KONRAD ADENAUER
ALEXANDER THE GREAT
SALVADOR ALLENDE
MARC ANTONY
CORAZON AQUINO
YASIR ARAFAT
KING ARTHUR
HAFEZ AL-ASSAD
KEMAL ATATÜRK
ATTILA
CLEMENT ATTLEE
AUGUSTUS CAESAR
MENACHEM BEGIN
DAVID BEN-GURION
OTTO VON BISMARCK
LÉON BLUM
SIMON BOLÍVAR
CESARE BORGIA
WILLY BRANDT
LEONID BREZHNEV
JULIUS CAESAR
JOHN CALVIN
JIMMY CARTER
FIDEL CASTRO
CATHERINE THE GREAT
CHARLEMAGNE
CHIANG KAI-SHEK
WINSTON CHURCHILL
GEORGES CLEMENCEAU
CLEOPATRA
CONSTANTINE THE GREAT
HERNÁN CORTÉS
OLIVER CROMWELL
GEORGES-JACQUES
   DANTON
JEFFERSON DAVIS
MOSHE DAYAN
CHARLES DE GAULLE
EAMON DE VALERA
EUGENE DEBS
DENG XIAOPING
BENJAMIN DISRAELI
ALEXANDER DUBČEK
FRANÇOIS & JEAN-CLAUDE
   DUVALIER
DWIGHT EISENHOWER
ELEANOR OF AQUITAINE
ELIZABETH I
FAISAL
FERDINAND & ISABELLA
FRANCISCO FRANCO
BENJAMIN FRANKLIN

FREDERICK THE GREAT
INDIRA GANDHI
MOHANDAS GANDHI
GIUSEPPE GARIBALDI
AMIN & BASHIR GEMAYEL
GENGHIS KHAN
WILLIAM GLADSTONE
MIKHAIL GORBACHEV
ULYSSES S. GRANT
ERNESTO "CHE" GUEVARA
TENZIN GYATSO
ALEXANDER HAMILTON
DAG HAMMARSKJÖLD
HENRY VIII
HENRY OF NAVARRE
PAUL VON HINDENBURG
HIROHITO
ADOLF HITLER
HO CHI MINH
KING HUSSEIN
IVAN THE TERRIBLE
ANDREW JACKSON
JAMES I
WOJCIECH JARUZELSKI
THOMAS JEFFERSON
JOAN OF ARC
POPE JOHN XXIII
POPE JOHN PAUL II
LYNDON JOHNSON
BENITO JUÁREZ
JOHN KENNEDY
ROBERT KENNEDY
JOMO KENYATTA
AYATOLLAH KHOMEINI
NIKITA KHRUSHCHEV
KIM IL SUNG
MARTIN LUTHER KING, JR.
HENRY KISSINGER
KUBLAI KHAN
LAFAYETTE
ROBERT E. LEE
VLADIMIR LENIN
ABRAHAM LINCOLN
DAVID LLOYD GEORGE
LOUIS XIV
MARTIN LUTHER
JUDAS MACCABEUS
JAMES MADISON
NELSON & WINNIE
   MANDELA
MAO ZEDONG
FERDINAND MARCOS
GEORGE MARSHALL

MARY, QUEEN OF SCOTS
TOMÁS MASARYK
GOLDA MEIR
KLEMENS VON METTERNICH
JAMES MONROE
HOSNI MUBARAK
ROBERT MUGABE
BENITO MUSSOLINI
NAPOLÉON BONAPARTE
GAMAL ABDEL NASSER
JAWAHARLAL NEHRU
NERO
NICHOLAS II
RICHARD NIXON
KWAME NKRUMAH
DANIEL ORTEGA
MOHAMMED REZA PAHLAVI
THOMAS PAINE
CHARLES STEWART
   PARNELL
PERICLES
JUAN PERÓN
PETER THE GREAT
POL POT
MUAMMAR EL-QADDAFI
RONALD REAGAN
CARDINAL RICHELIEU
MAXIMILIEN ROBESPIERRE
ELEANOR ROOSEVELT
FRANKLIN ROOSEVELT
THEODORE ROOSEVELT
ANWAR SADAT
HAILE SELASSIE
PRINCE SIHANOUK
JAN SMUTS
JOSEPH STALIN
SUKARNO
SUN YAT-SEN
TAMERLANE
MOTHER TERESA
MARGARET THATCHER
JOSIP BROZ TITO
TOUSSAINT L'OUVERTURE
LEON TROTSKY
PIERRE TRUDEAU
HARRY TRUMAN
QUEEN VICTORIA
LECH WALESA
GEORGE WASHINGTON
CHAIM WEIZMANN
WOODROW WILSON
XERXES
EMILIANO ZAPATA
ZHOU ENLAI

CHELSEA HOUSE PUBLISHERS

ON LEADERSHIP
Arthur M. Schlesinger, jr.

LEADERSHIP, it may be said, is really what makes the world go round. Love no doubt smooths the passage; but love is a private transaction between consenting adults. Leadership is a public transaction with history. The idea of leadership affirms the capacity of individuals to move, inspire and mobilize masses of people so that they act together in pursuit of an end. Sometimes leadership serves good purposes, sometimes bad; but whether the end is benign or evil, great leaders are those men and women who leave their personal stamp on history.

Now, the very concept of leadership implies the proposition that individuals can make a difference. This proposition has never been universally accepted. From classical times to the present day, eminent thinkers have regarded individuals as no more than the agents and pawns of larger forces, whether the gods and goddesses of the ancient world or, in the modern era, race, class, nation, the dialectic, the will of the people, the spirit of the times, history itself. Against such forces, the individual dwindles into insignificance.

So contends the thesis of historical determinism. Tolstoy's great novel *War and Peace* offers a famous statement of the case. Why, Tolstoy asked, did millions of men in the Napoleonic wars, denying their human feelings and their common sense, move back and forth across Europe slaughtering their fellows? "The war," Tolstoy answered, "was bound to happen simply because it was bound to happen." All prior history predetermined it. As for leaders, they, Tolstoy said, "are but the labels that serve to give a name to an end and, like labels, they have the least possible connection with the event." The greater the leader, "the more conspicuous the inevitability and the predestination of every act he commits." The leader, said Tolstoy, is "the slave of history."

Determinism takes many forms. Marxism is the determinism of class, Nazism the determinism of race. But the idea of men and women as the slaves of history runs athwart the deepest human instincts. Rigid determinism abolishes the idea of human freedom—the assumption of free choice that underlies every move we make, every word we speak, every thought we think. It abolishes the idea of human responsibility, since it is manifestly unfair to reward or punish people for actions that are by definition beyond their control. No one can live consistently by any deterministic creed. The Marxist states prove this themselves by their extreme susceptibility to the cult of leadership.

More than that, history refutes the idea that individuals make no difference. In December 1931 a British politician crossing Park Avenue in New York City between 76th and 77th Streets around ten-thirty at night looked in the wrong direction and was knocked down by an automobile—a moment, he later recalled, of a man aghast, a world aglare: "I do not understand why I was not broken like an eggshell or squashed like a gooseberry." Fourteen months later an American politician, sitting in an open car in Miami, Florida, was fired on by an assassin; the man beside him was hit. Those who believe that individuals make no difference to history might well ponder whether the next two decades would have been the same had Mario Contasini's car killed Winston Churchill in 1931 and Giuseppe Zangara's bullet killed Franklin Roosevelt in 1933. Suppose, in addition, that Adolf Hitler had been killed in the street fighting during the Munich *Putsch* of 1923 and that Lenin had died of typhus during the First World War. What would the 20th century be like now?

For better or for worse, individuals do make a difference. "The notion that a people can run itself and its affairs anonymously," wrote the philosopher William James, "is now well known to be the silliest of absurdities. Mankind does nothing save through initiatives on the part of inventors, great or small, and imitation by the rest of us—these are the sole factors in human progress. Individuals of genius show the way, and set the patterns, which common people then adopt and follow."

Leadership, James suggests, means leadership in thought as well as in action. In the long run, leaders in thought may well make the greater difference to the world. But, as Woodrow Wilson once said, "Those only are leaders of men, in the general eye, who lead in action. . . . It is at their hands that new thought gets its translation into the crude language of deeds." Leaders in thought often invent in solitude and obscurity, leaving to later generations the tasks of imitation. Leaders in action—the leaders portrayed in this series— have to be effective in their own time.

And they cannot be effective by themselves. They must act in response to the rhythms of their age. Their genius must be adapted, in a phrase of William James's, "to the receptivities of the moment." Leaders are useless without followers. "There goes the mob," said the French politician hearing a clamor in the streets. "I am their leader. I must follow them." Great leaders turn the inchoate emotions of the mob to purposes of their own. They seize on the opportunities of their time, the hopes, fears, frustrations, crises, potentialities.

They succeed when events have prepared the way for them, when the community is waiting to be aroused, when they can provide the clarifying and organizing ideas. Leadership ignites the circuit between the individual and the mass and thereby alters history.

It may alter history for better or for worse. Leaders have been responsible for the most extravagant follies and most monstrous crimes that have beset suffering humanity. They have also been vital in such gains as humanity has made in individual freedom, religious and racial tolerance, social justice and respect for human rights.

There is no sure way to tell in advance who is going to lead for good and who for evil. But a glance at the gallery of men and women in *World Leaders—Past and Present* suggests some useful tests.

One test is this: do leaders lead by force or by persuasion? By command or by consent? Through most of history leadership was exercised by the divine right of authority. The duty of followers was to defer and to obey. "Theirs not to reason why,/ Theirs but to do and die." On occasion, as with the so-called "enlightened despots" of the 18th century in Europe, absolutist leadership was animated by humane purposes. More often, absolutism nourished the passion for domination, land, gold and conquest and resulted in tyranny.

The great revolution of modern times has been the revolution of equality. The idea that all people should be equal in their legal condition has undermined the old structures of authority, hierarchy and deference. The revolution of equality has had two contrary effects on the nature of leadership. For equality, as Alexis de Tocqueville pointed out in his great study *Democracy in America*, might mean equality in servitude as well as equality in freedom.

"I know of only two methods of establishing equality in the political world," Tocqueville wrote. "Rights must be given to every citizen, or none at all to anyone . . . save one, who is the master of all." There was no middle ground "between the sovereignty of all and the absolute power of one man." In his astonishing prediction of 20th-century totalitarian dictatorship, Tocqueville explained how the revolution of equality could lead to the "*Führerprinzip*" and more terrible absolutism than the world had ever known.

But when rights are given to every citizen and the sovereignty of all is established, the problem of leadership takes a new form, becomes more exacting than ever before. It is easy to issue commands and enforce them by the rope and the stake, the concentration camp and the *gulag*. It is much harder to use argument and achievement to overcome opposition and win consent. The Founding Fathers of the United States understood the difficulty. They believed that history had given them the opportunity to decide, as

Alexander Hamilton wrote in the first Federalist Paper, whether men are indeed capable of basing government on "reflection and choice, or whether they are forever destined to depend . . . on accident and force."

Government by reflection and choice called for a new style of leadership and a new quality of followership. It required leaders to be responsive to popular concerns, and it required followers to be active and informed participants in the process. Democracy does not eliminate emotion from politics; sometimes it fosters demagoguery; but it is confident that, as the greatest of democratic leaders put it, you cannot fool all of the people all of the time. It measures leadership by results and retires those who overreach or falter or fail.

It is true that in the long run despots are measured by results too. But they can postpone the day of judgment, sometimes indefinitely, and in the meantime they can do infinite harm. It is also true that democracy is no guarantee of virtue and intelligence in government, for the voice of the people is not necessarily the voice of God. But democracy, by assuring the rights of opposition, offers built-in resistance to the evils inherent in absolutism. As the theologian Reinhold Niebuhr summed it up, "Man's capacity for justice makes democracy possible, but man's inclination to injustice makes democracy necessary."

A second test for leadership is the end for which power is sought. When leaders have as their goal the supremacy of a master race or the promotion of totalitarian revolution or the acquisition and exploitation of colonies or the protection of greed and privilege or the preservation of personal power, it is likely that their leadership will do little to advance the cause of humanity. When their goal is the abolition of slavery, the liberation of women, the enlargement of opportunity for the poor and powerless, the extension of equal rights to racial minorities, the defense of the freedoms of expression and opposition, it is likely that their leadership will increase the sum of human liberty and welfare.

Leaders have done great harm to the world. They have also conferred great benefits. You will find both sorts in this series. Even "good" leaders must be regarded with a certain wariness. Leaders are not demigods; they put on their trousers one leg after another just like ordinary mortals. No leader is infallible, and every leader needs to be reminded of this at regular intervals. Irreverence irritates leaders but is their salvation. Unquestioning submission corrupts leaders and demeans followers. Making a cult of a leader is always a mistake. Fortunately hero worship generates its own antidote. "Every hero," said Emerson, "becomes a bore at last."

The signal benefit the great leaders confer is to embolden the rest of us to live according to our own best selves, to be active, insistent, and resolute in affirming our own sense of things. For great leaders attest to the reality of human freedom against the supposed inevitabilities of history. And they attest to the wisdom and power that may lie within the most unlikely of us, which is why Abraham Lincoln remains the supreme example of great leadership. A great leader, said Emerson, exhibits new possibilities to all humanity. "We feed on genius. . . . Great men exist that there may be greater men."

Great leaders, in short, justify themselves by emancipating and empowering their followers. So humanity struggles to master its destiny, remembering with Alexis de Tocqueville: "It is true that around every man a fatal circle is traced beyond which he cannot pass; but within the wide verge of that circle he is powerful and free; as it is with man, so with communities."

—*New York*

1

In His Father's Footsteps

It was a blustery winter morning in the year 754. The wind ripped through the foothills of the Alps. The young prince had spent many days now tramping through the vast frozen fields and wild forests that made up his father's kingdom. Yet the tingling he felt was due not to cold but to excitement. Today he would meet the pope.

This was the first time in history that a pope had left Rome and crossed the Alps to visit a king of Frankland, the land occupied in modern times by parts of France, Germany, the Netherlands, and Belgium. And Charles had been entrusted with the job of greeting the pope and guiding him on the last leg of his journey.

The tiny specks far off in the snow began to grow larger. One glimmered and sparkled like a brilliant jewel. Charles had heard that the pope dressed in radiant cloth of gold. Could it be. . .?

The prince pulled back his shoulders and stood as tall as he could. Though only 11, he could pass for a grown man when he tried. And today more than ever he wanted to look the part of a king. Charles was fiercely proud of his father, the king known as Pepin "the Short," who was renowned

---

Charles the Great, or Charlemagne (742–814), was crowned in a traditional Frankish ritual that called for the king-elect to be raised by his nobles on a shield. The leather-covered, wooden shield symbolized the ruler's willingness to fight and, if necessary, to die for his people.

Charles's father, Pepin the Short (714–768), inherited the position of mayor of the palace, or actual ruler of the Franks. Wanting to be king in rank as well as in power, Pepin seized the Frankish throne in 751. His reign lasted 17 years.

13

King Clovis I (466—511) receives his Christian baptism in 496, 15 years after his accession to the Salian Frankish throne. Subsequent to his conversion, he laid the foundations of a long and close relationship between the Franks and the Roman Catholic church.

for his able, just, and courageous rule. Now Charles wanted to make an impression on Pope Stephen II that would do the Frankish crown justice. Nervously, he straightened the gold clasp that held his great fur cloak.

But as the travelers came nearer, all the boy's thoughts of kingly dignity left him. He was spellbound by the awesome figure approaching. Sunlight danced between the gold robe and the brilliant white snow. The thought came to him: What was a mere earthly king next to this man? What could compare with being the head of the kingdom of God on earth?

Charles had long looked forward to the time when he would be king, when he would have the chance to serve his people with courage and justice as his father had done. That day in the Alps, a second dream took root in him as well. He would be a new kind of king, one who would serve his God and his church above all.

Three centuries before Pepin became king of the Franks, the Roman Empire, long under attack by barbarian tribes, had virtually ceased to exist. By the time Charles met the pope in the Alps, Europe's only unified kingdom was Frankland, which had been established and expanded by a fifth-century Christian king named Clovis.

Clovis's descendants had worn the crown of the Franks for 240 years. These rulers, however, had become more inept with each generation, and by the early 700s, they were kings in name only. The men who really ruled were hereditary administrators called mayors of the palace. It was they who controlled the country's economy and its militia, they who were respected and followed by the people.

Finally, in 751, the church put its authority behind Frankland's mayor of the palace—who was Pepin, Charles's father. "It is better," said Pope Zacharias, "to give the name of king to him who has the wisdom and the power rather than to him who has only the name of king without authority." Saying this, the pope had the old king, Childeric III, sent to a monastery and Pepin crowned king of the Franks.

Pepin's crowning changed the nature of kingship in Frankland. Until then, although they were Christian, the Frankish kings had been much like pagan rulers. They owed their crowns to their ancient bloodlines. But Pepin owed his to the grace of God. He had been chosen by the church. He came to see support and defense of the church as being as much his duty as defense of his own people. His relationship with the popes was an especially close one. Throughout his life he exchanged warm letters with Rome. Pope Stephen II, who had succeeded Zacharias, was godfather to Pepin's sons and regularly sent these two boys extravagant presents.

Charles, Pepin's first son, was born in 742. From his earliest years the young prince was taught a

Charlemagne gave himself eagerly to riding and hunting, arts into which he was, as a Frank, born.
—EINHARD
recalling Charles's boyhood

Pope Zacharias (d. 752), eager to enlist the assistance of the Franks against his enemies in Italy, sanctioned Pepin's usurpation of the Frankish throne from King Childeric III (d. 754).

Frankish leader Charles Martel (688–741) strikes down a Saracen invader at the Battle of Tours in 732. Known as "The Hammer" because of his skill with the lethal iron weapon, Martel—who was Charles's grandfather—hoped to preserve European Christianity by stemming the Moslem Saracen incursions into the southwestern part of the continent.

deep love of the church. His mother, Queen Bertrada, was a deeply religious woman. His tutor headed one of the greatest monasteries in Europe. Charles must also have been impressed by the attentions his holy godfather showered on him and by the high regard his father had for the pope. Even before he was sent on his mission to greet Pope Stephen, Charles had acquired the devoutness that was to remain with him all his life.

Charles also learned from his father that support of the church involved more than exchanging letters and gifts. If needed, the king had to be willing to risk his subjects' lives in defense of the pope.

Pepin's loyalty to Pope Stephen was put to the test shortly after he was crowned. The pope had decided to visit the Frankish king for more than just a show of friendship. He had come to ask

Pepin's help against his threatening neighbors, the Lombards.

The Lombards, like the Franks, were a Germanic people. Years ago, the Franks and the Lombards had been friends and allies. However, Pepin's growing ties with the church were to change that. The recent Lombard kings were strong and ambitious men. Not content with the northern part of Italy they had originally occupied, they had established two important duchies—territories ruled by dukes—farther south. In between these two duchies was the city of Rome, where the pope lived. And now the Lombard king was threatening Rome as well.

Although he was still in his teens, Charles took an active part in the fighting in Italy, which checked the Lombard advance. He also helped his father put down a rebellion in Aquitaine, a province in the southeast part of Frankland (today, central France).

By the time Charles was 25, he had learned much about how to lead men. He had been in charge of a command of his own since he was 19. He had also

Childeric III steps down from the throne as Frankish nobles acknowledge the sovereignty of Pepin the Short (left of center, gripping spear). Pepin ordered Childeric shorn of the long hair that symbolized his royalty and forced the deposed monarch to enter a monastery, where he died three years later.

The empire inherited by Charles and his younger brother, Carloman (751–771), included most of present-day France, Belgium, and the Netherlands, as well as regions that are now part of West Germany and Switzerland.

acquired, in addition to his strong love of the church, a deep respect for higher culture—literature, science, and art. The traditions of the ancient Romans were of course still very much evident in Italy. Roman culture also continued to flourish in Aquitaine, which had been heavily settled by the Romans in the days of their vast empire hundreds of years earlier. Even though it was to do battle that he had visited both places, their civilized ways had made a lasting impression on Charles.

The three passions that had so early taken root in the young prince—his desire to rule men, his devotion to the church, and his love of culture— were to blend to make Charles one of the greatest kings Europe had ever known.

Simplified genealogical table of the Carolingians

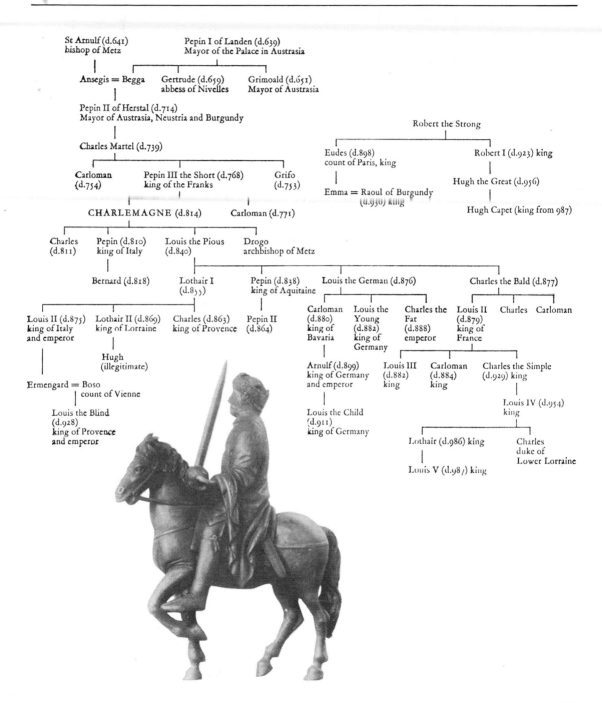

St Arnulf (d.641)
bishop of Metz

Pepin I of Landen (d.639)
Mayor of the Palace in Austrasia

Ansegis = Begga

Gertrude (d.659)
abbess of Nivelles

Grimoald (d.651)
Mayor of Austrasia

Pepin II of Herstal (d.714)
Mayor of Austrasia, Neustria and Burgundy

Robert the Strong

Charles Martel (d.739)

Eudes (d.898)
count of Paris, king

Robert I (d.923) king

Carloman
(d.754)

Pepin III the Short (d.768)
king of the Franks

Grifo
(d.753)

Emma = Raoul of Burgundy
(d.936) king

Hugh the Great (d.956)

CHARLEMAGNE (d.814)

Carloman (d.771)

Hugh Capet (king from 987)

Charles
(d.811)

Pepin (d.810)
king of Italy

Louis the Pious
(d.840)

Drogo
archbishop of Metz

Bernard (d.818)

Lothair I
(d.855)

Pepin (d.838)
king of Aquitaine

Louis the German (d.876)

Charles the Bald (d.877)

Louis II (d.875)
king of Italy
and emperor

Lothair II (d.869)
king of Lorraine

Charles (d.863)
king of Provence

Pepin II
(d.864)

Carloman
(d.880)
king of
Bavaria

Louis the
Young
(d.882)
king of
Germany

Charles the
Fat
(d.888)
emperor

Louis II
(d.879)
king of
France

Charles   Carloman

Hugh
(illegitimate)

Arnulf (d.899)
king of Germany
and emperor

Louis III
(d.882)
king

Carloman
(d.884)
king

Charles the Simple
(d.929) king

Ermengard = Boso
count of Vienne

Louis the Child
(d.911)
king of Germany

Louis IV (d.954)
king

Louis the Blind
(d.928)
king of Provence
and emperor

Lothair (d.986) king

Charles
duke of
Lower Lorraine

Louis V (d.987) king

19

2

Young and
Hot-Blooded King

To be a great ruler requires enormous energy and drive. It requires as well a real enjoyment of power. In young Charles these qualities were apparent at an early age, sometimes to excess.

Much of Charles's character could be read from his physical presence. He was a huge, strapping man—6 1/2 feet tall. He was in robust good health and radiated a sense of great vigor. This tremendous energy was in part a blessing Charles had enjoyed since birth. It was also due to healthy personal habits. He had a lusty appetite, but he never indulged to excess and was particularly moderate in drink. He also exercised daily. Oddly, Charles had a high-pitched voice that seemed out of place in a man his size. But there was little else about him that could detract from the imposing sense of strength, energy, and authority he projected naturally.

Charles more than looked the part of a ruler. Building and ruling were the essence of his soul. Charles was also, it seemed, born to rule alone. From an early age he showed a reluctance to share power with another.

In 768 King Pepin died, leaving his kingdom to his two sons, Charles and his younger brother, Carloman. The policy of dividing a kingdom among

In an engraving made several centuries after his death, Charles is portrayed with the emblems of his kingship: a jeweled crown, a sword, and an orb. The royal orb—a globe surmounted by a cross—symbolized the supremacy of God over the ruler's earthly kingdom.

Many authorities believe that this ninth-century bronze statue portrays Charles. Clearly a king, the mounted figure wears typically Frankish clothing: a long riding cloak, a tunic, and hose.

children rather than leaving it to the oldest was an old Frankish custom. Thus, Charles was to share the rule of Frankland with his brother. From the beginning this led to tensions.

The same year Pepin died, the Aquitainians rose again in revolt. Charles decided to march off at once with just the small group of men he had with him, not even waiting to call up the services of his lords. He assumed his brother, who, like him, was in charge of half of Aquitaine, would help. Carloman, however, was an indecisive, weak-willed young man, jealous of his older brother's talents as a leader. He spitefully refused to send aid and Charles found himself forced to confront the Aquitainians alone. Despite the unfavorable odds, the brave and daring young king subdued the revolt in just two months.

Actually, Charles probably relished having the challenge all to himself. Yet, in the aftermath, resentment lingered, and there were rumors of war between the two brothers.

A twist of fate, however, kept the festering hostility from breaking out in actual fighting: In 771, at the age of 22, Carloman suddenly died. With Carloman's death, Charles ruled Frankland alone.

From his earliest years Charles had been a deeply affectionate man. Yet, as his relationship with his brother showed, even with those he loved deeply, the young king had a need to dominate.

In the Frankland of the 700s, parents usually arranged the marriages of their offspring. King Pepin and Queen Bertrada had arranged two marriages for their oldest son while he was in his early twenties. Charles's first wife, a Frankish princess named Himiltrude, bore him a hunchbacked son named Pepin, who was later declared illegitimate. His second wife, Desideria, the daughter of the cultured king of the Lombards, was too intellectual and independent for his taste. Charles quickly divorced both these young women. (The divorce laws were less strict than they were to become later in the Middle Ages.) Charles wanted to choose for himself an appropriate wife.

At last he got his chance. His third wife, Hildegarde, was a woman he could truly love. She was

> *Although the reason for undertaking the war was similar to that which had inspired his father . . . it is clear that Charlemagne fought it with much more energy and brought it to a different conclusion.*
>
> —EINHARD
> on Charles's war with the Lombards

This imaginary group portrait shows Charles and four of his five wives, probably Himiltrude, Hildegarde, Fastrada, and Liutgard.

an ideal mate for Charles. She was only 13 when they married and seemed never to lose the quiet, yielding ways of girlhood. She was happiest simply looking after her family, and often accompanied her husband on his many travels.

Yet, for all their closeness, Hildegarde seldom involved herself in affairs of state. She was content to let her husband reign supreme. Also, to Charles's great pleasure, Hildegarde had a hearty, lusty nature to match his own. She gave him five daughters and four sons.

Now 30 years old, happily married, and in control of the entire Frankish kingdom, Charles turned his attention to border problems with the Saxons. Also a Germanic people, the Saxons were tall, golden-haired, and strong. But unlike most of the Germanic tribes who had overrun the Roman Empire and the areas bordering it, they had largely escaped contact with the Romans and the civilizing influence such contact might have had on them and their culture. They were known throughout Europe for their pagan, warlike spirit, and for their fearlessness as fighters. The Saxons' land bordered the kingdom of the Franks on the east, and an almost continual state of war had existed between the two peoples for hundreds of years.

For the last 15 years of Pepin's reign there had been peace along the Saxon border, but that was the calm before the storm. In 772 hostilities again surfaced. Although no one foresaw it at the time, those first, seemingly small-scale encounters were to be the beginning of the longest, most savage war of the new king's reign.

The Saxons provoked the first Frankish campaign against them by burning a church. However, Charles had only needed an excuse to fight. For he was eager to show what his army could do and he knew that only a great challenge could produce a strong sense of pride and unity among his men. Saxony was the opportunity for which he had been waiting. Equally important to the king was the religious aspect of the brewing conflict. He dreamed of converting the pagan Saxons to Christianity.

On hearing of the Saxon church-burning, Charles promptly called together his council of lords and got their permission to wage war. His first campaign, in 772, was a modest one, its purpose mainly

The quick-thinking Hildegarde prepares to kill a wild bull that has gored Charles's horse during a hunting expedition. The hunt, which provided food as well as exciting sport, was a favorite pastime of the royal couple.

Avenging himself upon the Saxons for their burning of Christian churches, Charles orders the toppling of the Irminsul, a huge, intricately carved tree trunk that played an important role in the Saxons' pagan religion.

symbolic. Frankish troops destroyed the center of Saxon worship: the Irminsul, a huge tree trunk that represented one of their gods. The Saxons surrendered quickly and promised good behavior. All was resolved in time for Charles to return home to Hildegarde and share with her the birth of their first son.

Trouble, however, soon appeared on another front, caused in part by one of Charles's earlier marriages. His union with the Lombard princess had been part of a grand scheme of the new king of the Lombards, Desiderius, to undo Pepin's curbs on his people. Desiderius, like the earlier Lombard kings, was an ambitious man. He had never turned over all the lands the Lombards had promised Pepin they would surrender to the pope. And not only did he intend to hold onto his old territory, he planned to enlarge it. The only obstacle was the Franks, who had sworn to protect the pope. By marrying his daughter to a young Frankish prince, Desiderius had hoped to soften their attitude toward the Lombards. When Charles sent the princess home he

Typical of the finely crafted religious objects created by Lombard master goldsmiths in the eighth century, this jewel-encrusted cross was made for Desiderius (d. 774), who ruled Lombardy from 756 until his capture and deposition by Charles in 773. Charles's troops brought many such pieces back to Frankland after they defeated the Lombards.

unknowingly thwarted Desiderius's plans, and the Lombard king grew angry.

In 773, just two years after he had become king of all the Franks, Charles received an urgent request from Rome. There was a new Lombard threat, and the pope pleaded for the help of the Franks. Charles took the request before his council of lords. As would happen many times over, the lords were easily persuaded. They voted for war.

Charles was a born conqueror. Though not famous for his skill as a warrior or for brave exploits on the battlefield, he had a genius for organizing and inspiring his troops.

Victory in the early Middle Ages depended to a large degree on speed and numbers, and Charles had a great talent for moving men. When he called up his subjects to fight, no excuses were tolerated. There was a penalty for showing up even one day late. As there were no maps, marching men to the site of battle required keen instincts and extensive knowledge of terrain. Charles was blessed with both. Also, his great energy enabled him to maintain a grueling pace. Inspired by their king's example, his men followed suit.

Now, as in Aquitaine, Charles wasted no time getting the campaign under way. Many of his men grumbled at the prospect of crossing the Alps, but their king was determined. Within months, the Frankish soldiers were taking one Lombard city after another until soon only one, Pavia, still held out. In 773 Charles attacked the city, but had his men prepare for a long siege. Pavia was well fortified and Charles was not about to waste lives on a reckless, all-out assault.

Leaving part of his army at Pavia, Charles made his first visit to Rome. As a devout pilgrim, he had expected to be impressed by the Holy City. But when he arrived in Rome, he was overwhelmed. Banners waved. Long lines of Roman militia snapped salutes. Schoolchildren sang hymns. Charles was eager to meet the man who had arranged such a lavish greeting.

Hadrian I, who had succeeded to the Throne of St. Peter in 772, was descended from the ancient

Roman aristocracy. His noble lineage was evident in his generous style and courteous manner. Not only did he greet the king of the Franks with full pomp, he also treated him to elaborate banquets and entertainments.

More important to Charles, Hadrian also had a Roman nobleman's strong, upright character, a love of culture, a keen, well-trained intellect, and a deep and sincere love of the church. Charles was completely won over by the new pope's piety and great personal warmth.

Back in Pavia, Charles and his men finally defeated the Lombards after a nine-month siege. Until now Charles had been following closely in his father's footsteps. Pepin had subdued a rebellion in Aquitaine and defeated the troops of Lombardy, and now his eldest son had done likewise. But with his Lombard victory the new king showed he had ideas and a style of his own.

Pepin had been content with promises of peace from the Lombards. Not so his son. Charles was interested in permanent peace, which he equated with complete conquest. He had no intention of letting the Lombards off with promises only to find himself crossing the Alps again in two years, as his father had been forced to do. He decided to take over the Lombard kingdom and make the conquered land a part of Frankland. In 774 Charles had himself crowned king of the Lombards and the Franks.

After Charles had conquered the Lombards, Pope

En route to Lombardy in 773, Charles and his men fight their way across the Alps. Although few of the Franks were experienced in mountain warfare, they quickly overcame the Lombard defenders and marched on to King Desiderius's stronghold, the walled city of Pavia.

Hadrian I (d. 795), the pope who welcomed Charles to Rome in 773, greeting the Frankish king at the top of the stairs of St. Peter's Basilica. Charles, reverently following the custom of other pilgrims, fell to his knees and kissed each step as he approached the pontiff.

ADRIANVS NATION
CIMBRICVS PATRIA
DERTVNENSIS P

Hadrian requested some of the former Lombard lands. Eager to honor his new friend's wishes, Charles responded generously. This served to make the relationship between the church and the Frankish king even stronger.

Charles did not linger long in Italy, however. His loyalty to both family and country called him home. He had received word that the infant daughter recently born to Hildegard had died, and he longed to be with his wife in her mourning. He was also needed on another battlefield—there were reports that the formidable Saxons were acting up again, more seriously than ever.

Traditionally the Saxons had no king; instead, each small clan had its own chief. In the past, this lack of unity had prevented them from posing a serious threat to Frankland.

But that old state of affairs was changing. A strong and intelligent leader had emerged from among the many Saxon chiefs, and he was attempting to unite his people. The new leader's name was Widukind.

Charles decided to act at once. Early in 775 he summoned together an army and marched to Saxony. His speed caught the enemy off guard, and the Franks took the Saxon fort of Sigiburg in a single assault. The Saxons were skilled at guerrilla warfare, but in conventional battles their forces were no match for the Franks' well-organized army. Frankish cavalrymen, their swords at the ready, would sweep forward in close formation, their thunderous charges backed by a lethal moving wall of archers and spear-thrusting infantrymen. Charles continued to score victory after victory.

The Franks hounded the Saxons for the next two years, and each victory was followed by an attempt to convert those conquered to Christianity. Many of the vanquished were forced to undergo baptism. At this point in his career Charles had not yet learned that no true religious conversion can be brought about by force.

By 777 Widukind had given up and fled to Denmark, where the king of the Danes offered him refuge. Charles decided that his work in Saxony

Mounted on his magnificent charger, Charles sternly oversees the forcible baptism of defeated Saxon soldiers in 775. A chronicler of the period declared that Charles was determined to fight the Saxons "until they were conquered and converted to the Christian religion, or totally annihilated."

was complete, but, as in Lombardy, he was not content with just booty and oaths from the conquered people. They would become a part of his realm. Charles built a great fort near the Saxon town of Paderborn and there, in 777, held the annual assembly of the Franks. On witnessing the pageantry of their new ruler's court, the Saxons were greatly awed. Afterward, many of them gave up their old gods (who were similar to those worshiped by the ancient Greeks and Romans) and presented themselves voluntarily for baptism.

For Charles it was a moment of great triumph. It now seemed that no challenge was beyond him. He had finally put an end to the Lombard threat to the pope, something his father had been unable to do after years of trying. And he had won for the church vast new territories and thousands of new souls, among them the most stubborn pagans in Europe. God, it seemed, was on his side.

Yet, for all his devoutness, Charles was subject to the lure of pride that is so often a special temptation for the young, strong, and gifted. From the eyes now so proudly surveying victory, bitter tears would soon fall.

The Saxons returned to paganism like a dog that returns to its vomit.
—Frankish chronicler

29

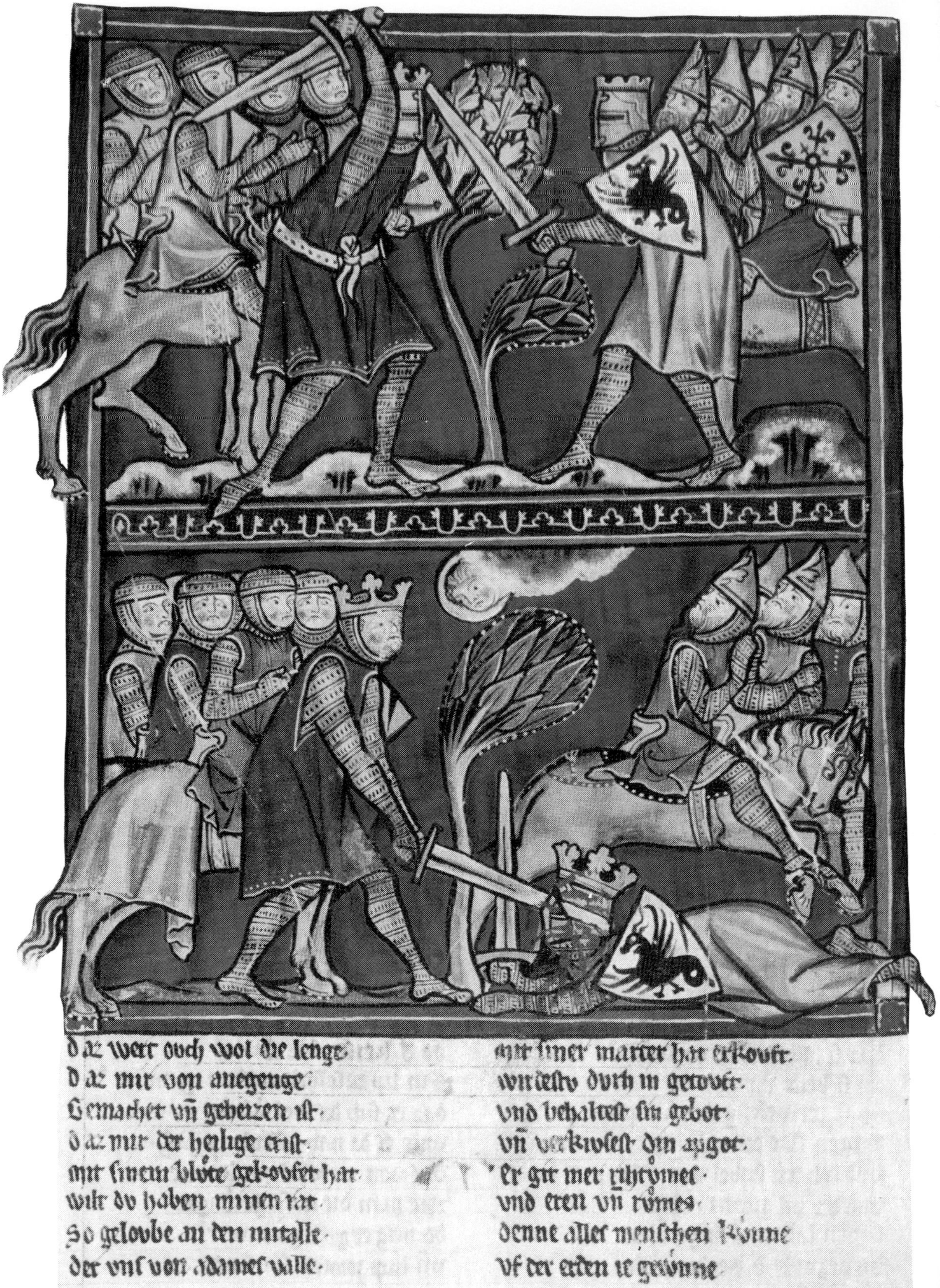

daz wert ouch wol die lenge·
daz mir von anegenge·
Gemachet vñ geheizen ist·
daz mir der heilige crist·
mit sinem blúte gekoufet hat·
wilt dv haben minen rat·
So geloube an den mit alle·
der vns von adames valle·

mit siner marter hat erkovft·
wiltestv dvrch in getovft·
vnd behaltest sin gebot·
vñ verkiusest din apgot·
er git mir rhtvmer·
vnd eren vñ rómes·
denne aller menschen kúnne·
vf der erden ie gewúnne

3

Defeat and Despair

Frankish warriors on the march were an impressive sight, with their golden-haired, unhelmeted heads, their taut, strong bodies garbed in leather vests or light armor, their swords glittering in the sunlight. The sword was a Frank's principal, often his only, weapon, and much care was lavished on it. Its scabbard might be of silver or gold, perhaps studded with jewels. All of this contributed to the Frankish soldiers' air of proud strength and bright self-assurance.

Especially after his recent string of triumphs—in Aquitaine, Lombardy, and now Saxony—it seemed to Charles that his army was unbeatable. It was in this confident mood in 777 that the king greeted a strange group of foreigners who came to the meeting at Paderborn to ask a favor of him.

The foreign ambassadors must have aroused some suspicion among the Franks, for their heads were turbaned and they wore floor-length robes of elaborate silks. They were Moslems from Spain. (Although many Christians still lived in Spain, at this time the country was largely controlled by Moslems.)

The group that had come to seek Charles's help was loyal to the caliph of Baghdad, the central Moslem ruler. The group's leader, the governor of Barcelona, wanted to overthrow the Moslem emir of Cordoba, as he was defiant of the caliph.

At some other time Charles might have been

This portrait of Charles in elaborate royal robes was painted by the famous German artist Albrecht Dürer (1471–1528) in the late 15th century. In actuality, the Frankish king disliked ostentatious clothing, preferring simple linen garments similar to those worn by the majority of his subjects.

This illustration from a medieval manuscript shows (upper section) a battle being decided by one-on-one combat between Charles (left) and a Saracen knight. The knight's followers flee (lower section) after Charles kills their leader.

more hesitant about committing his men to a cause that seemed so remote from the interests of his people. But not now. By playing on the king's taste for conquest, the governor persuaded him easily. He promised the Frankish king several cities in return for his assistance. And Charles hoped to liberate the Christians of Spain from Moslem rule.

Charles prepared better for this campaign than he had for any other to date, for the fierceness of the Moslem soldiers was legendary. Charles's grandfather, Charles Martel, had repulsed the cav-

alry troops of the fanatical Moslem leader, Abd-ar-Rahman, in 732 at the Battle of Tours, a victory that had saved much of Europe for the Christian faith. So Charles assembled the largest army he could, calling up the best men from all parts of his territory. Then, feeling strong and optimistic, he set out for Spain. The year was 778.

Things seemed to go wrong from the very start. Charles succeeded in taking a few cities, but at great cost. He had counted on the help of Spanish Christians, assuming they would be eager for liber-

Roncesvalles (near top of map, between Bayonne and Pamplona) became the scene of one of history's most famous battles when the rear guard of Charles's army was ambushed and destroyed by the mountain Basques in 778. The stunning defeat inspired many legends and poems, including the celebrated *Song of Roland*, written in praise of the Frankish count whose pride prevented him from allowing his men to summon assistance.

ation, but he found them unenthusiastic about the Frankish cause. In fact, his army's advance was resisted by the Basques of the Pyrenees, the mountains that separate Spain from France. Angered, Charles destroyed the walls of the Basque city of Pampeluna. Nor did many Moslems appear eager to overthrow their present leader. The Moslem governor of Saragossa was unable to deliver that important city to the Franks, as he had promised. So after several months, the sobered king decided to order a retreat. His decision was strengthened by the news that the Saxons were once again causing trouble at home. The soldiers were hungry and tired as they marched back to the Pyrenees, but there was still much swagger in their manner. The terrain became increasingly forbidding as they approached the mountains. The woods were thick and jagged cliffs jutted up steeply, hemming them in on either side of the narrow passage. Yet their blustery good spirits continued. The cowed air of defeated men was not for them, nor was fear of dark forests. After all, they were Franks.

A sober fearlessness might have served them better. One evening, while pitching camp in the narrow pass at Roncesvalles, the Frankish army's rear guard heard a strange rumbling sound above them. Suddenly a huge boulder tumbled down the cliff and tore into one of the supply wagons. In minutes, the perplexed soldiers were overrun by a band of fierce Basque guerrillas, intent on revenging Charles's razing of their city's walls. The Franks tried to fend off the attackers, but their great swords were useless against the crafty Basques, who continued their barrage of boulders and arrows from the mountainside. The Franks might have summoned help from their forward ranks, but pride prevented anyone from blowing on the horn used for this purpose until it was too late.

By the time Charles, who had been at the front of the column, arrived, it was all over. A ghostly stillness had settled over the pass, pierced by just a

Enthroned at Paderborn, Charles informs the envoys of the caliph of Baghdad, Harun al-Rashid (764—809), that he will assist them in driving a rival Moslem leader from Spain. Like his grandfather, Charles Martel ("The Hammer"), Charles was eager to reconquer Spain for the Christian faith.

A treacherous knight named Ganelon kneels at the feet of King Charles before the Battle of Roncesvalles. According to the *Song of Roland*—a work of great literary, but dubious historical value—Ganelon engineered the destruction of Roland by telling the enemy that Charles's peace overtures were insincere, thus provoking the bloody ambush.

In Roncesvalles Charles now has set his feet / And for the dead he finds begins to weep.... / He sees his nephew lying on the green grass. / No wonder, then, that Charles is full of wrath. / Dismounts and goes to him; his heart is sad. / He holds the count between his own two hands / And on the body faints, so sharp's the pang.

—from the 11th-century epic
The Song of Roland

Charles was firm and steady in his human relationships, developing friendships easily, keeping it up with care and doing everything he possibly could for anyone whom he had admitted to this degree of intimacy.

—EINHARD

few feeble moans. Bodies of horses and men were strewn wildly about, stripped of their precious swords, mangled by rocks. Among them lay the remains of destroyed supply carts.

The king walked silently among the bodies, stopping frequently to kneel and weep beside those he recognized. The familiar faces were too numerous to count. The rear guard had included all the king's counts, or commanders, and to Charles they were more than commanders. They were friends. He had fought with them, hunted with them, feasted with them, loved them. And now they were dead.

Charles left the scene with a heaviness of heart he had never known before. He wondered how he had offended his God to deserve such punishment. Nor were his troubles to end at Roncesvalles.

While Charles was away in Spain, Hildegarde had given birth to twin sons, Louis and Lothar. The winter after Charles returned, Lothar died. And there were to be further military defeats as well.

Charles had ordered a retreat from Spain after he had learned of the latest violent activities of his formidable Saxon neighbors. Apparently the Franks' triumph of the preceding year was not nearly as conclusive as he had thought. In recent months Saxons had ravaged the fort Charles had built at Karlsburg, raided Frankish towns, burned churches, and massacred women and children. Worst of all, there were reports that Widukind had returned from Denmark. It was said he was behind this new wave of destruction.

In 782 Charles set about organizing a new Saxon offensive. He could see, however, that it was not the ideal moment for a campaign. Certain preparations were still needed. The Frankish counts who were to be in charge, though, had no patience for such thinking. Their hot tempers longed for vengeance. They could only see the great hordes of Saxons camped nearby at the base of Suntel Mountain. In defiance of orders, they decided to attack.

It was Roncesvalles all over again. In their overconfidence and their haste to do battle, the defiant counts did not wait for the necessary backup forces to arrive. They simply charged and the result was yet another horrible slaughter. Still more of the king's most noble and distinguished commanders were killed. Once again, pride in arms had led to a disaster for the Frankish army.

When he heard about the tragedy at Suntel Moun-

Count Roland, who was to meet his death at the Battle of Roncesvalles, is knighted by Charles as attendants attach spurs to the hero's ankles.

In a portrait carved on Charles's tomb at Aachen, the king grieves for his fallen soldiers. "In Roncesvalles," recounts the *Song of Roland*, "Charles now has set his feet, and for the dead he finds begins to weep."

Hooded monks conduct a mass for the Frankish soldiers slain at Roncesvalles. After the battle, Charles never again set foot in Spain, although he later sent his generals back to the Pyrenees, where they took possession of a strip of border territory called the Spanish March.

tain, something in the king snapped. His reaction to the massacre in Spain had been one of deep sadness and remorse, and for months Charles had searched his soul, asking himself what he might have done to bring on so cruel a fate for his people. Yet this time it was not grief but fury that enveloped the king. It was not atonement he desired, but revenge. His normal tolerance gave way to an unforgiving harshness that was not to lift for over 10 years.

To his camp at Verden (in what is now northern Germany) Charles summoned all the Saxon nobles who a year earlier had sworn loyalty to the Frankish realm. He demanded that they tell him the names of those who had been responsible for the recent rebellion. At first the nobles were silent, for such a request was contrary to all existing codes of honorable combat. It was considered as cruel to strip a man of his honor by forcing him to betray a fellow countryman as it was to take his life. But Charles was relentless, and after threatening the Saxon nobles with death, the king had the names of several thousand supposed traitors.

Charles summoned the accused before him, and within sight of their fellow Saxons he ordered them beheaded. In one day, nearly 4,500 Saxons perished and as many more were reduced to a state of groveling shame.

Although Charles could have counted Verden as a victory, it scarcely had the feel of one. It was not followed by rejoicing, but by a somber quiet. Eager as they had been for vengeance, Charles's subjects were shocked by the viciousness of their king.

Fast on the heels of Verden came more personal tragedy for Charles. In 783 both his mother and his beloved Hildegarde died. Though Charles soon remarried, his new queen, Fastrada, bore little semblance to the sweet, domestic Hildegarde. Rather, she was a whining and demanding woman who could do little to dispel the king's bitter mood. The sunny days of Charles's early reign—of gallant conquests and happy family life—seemed to be over.

Frankish troops escort a somber band of Saxons out of their ancestral territory. In punishment for their repeated uprisings, Charles ordered many thousands of Saxons removed from their homes and resettled in Frankland.

4

Years of Conquest

The next phase of Charles's empire-building was dominated by the cold, relentless spirit that was born of Roncesvalles and Verden. From 783 to 793 Charles and his army were almost ceaselessly on the march. At first their attention was focused on the Saxons, who, outraged by Charles's actions at Verden, had fought back furiously. The Franks matched them in their savagery. Though normally Charles did not fight during the winter months, from 783 to 785 he waged war year-round.

Finally, after three years of fierce and costly warfare that devastated the Saxon countryside and severely strained the resources of both sides, a victory of a new order appeared to be at hand. Widukind himself offered to surrender and accept the Christian faith. This was truly a momentous event, for both the Franks and the Saxons had long been awed by the Saxon chief's bravery, determination, and skill as a warrior.

Now, to spare his people further suffering, the great leader agreed to lay down his arms and renounce his pagan gods. Charles made elaborate preparations for the occasion, and he himself served as Widukind's godfather. After the baptism the king

The Frankish kingdom which Charles inherited from his father Pepin was already far-flung and powerful. By these wars of his he increased it to such an extent that he added to it almost as much again.
EINHARD

Duke Tassilo (742—794) gave this magnificent communion cup to the church after Charles ordered him banished to a monastery for the rest of his life. Art historians regard the chalice, with its image of Christ in inlaid silver, as a masterpiece.

Made more than five centuries after Charles's death, this jeweled, gold- and silverwork bust was designed to serve as a reliquary, or receptacle, for his skull. After Charles's body was exhumed in the year 1000, its bones were separated and placed in a number of such containers.

showered the famous new convert with gifts.

But these gestures of generosity were deceptive, for underlying them were the bitterness and distress that still gripped Charles. The king had not yet acknowledged the wrongfulness of the Verden slaughter. Nor had he sought forgiveness. He had simply buried his emotions under the strenuous demands of war. Consequently, he was unable to show his former enemies real mercy or forgiveness.

The terms decreed by the king for the defeated Saxons were harsh. In an important edict, called a capitulary, Charles spelled out a long list of actions that in Saxony were to be considered crimes. Of these, 15 carried the death penalty. Although this might not have seemed cruel in a later era, in Charles's day it was severe indeed, since in Frankish law very few crimes were punishable by death.

Worse still was the royal demand for tithes. A tithe, a contribution made to a religious institution, was traditionally supposed to be one-tenth of a person's income. A number of the king's advisors counseled against this measure, reminding him how difficult it would be for the Saxons to pay while still recovering from the ravages of war. They told him it would prevent the growth of the very thing he sought—genuine love of the church among the new converts. Charles, however, was deaf to their arguments.

Years later Charles would again pay on the battlefield for this severity, but for the present the Saxons were too devastated to raise anything but the most feeble protest. The king was at last free to turn his attention to other parts of his realm.

His next step in the consolidation of his kingdom was to crush, once and for all, the threat he sensed from the family of his old enemy, King Desiderius of Lombardy. Although the Franks had subdued the Lombards in 774, Desiderius's children were still at large. One son, Adalgis, had taken refuge with the Greeks in Constantinople. A daughter, Adalperga, was married to Arichis, the duke of Benevento in Italy. Another daughter, Liutperga, was married to Duke Tassilo of Bavaria, a region now part of West Germany. All three were proud of

How many battles were fought there and how much blood shed can still be seen by the deserted condition of Pannonia. The place where the palace of the Avar leader stood is so desolate that there is not so much as a trace of human habitation.

—EINHARD
on Charles's wars against the Avars

Dedistim&uentibufte signification&em
ut fugiant afacie arcuf:ll.

audime

Franks and Saxons meet in fierce hand-to-hand combat in the early 780s. The murderous efficiency of the bows and arrows, spears, and swords used in such battles inflicted enormous casualties on both sides.

their family's rich heritage and still resented seeing Lombardy swallowed up in the swelling Frankish kingdom.

Adalgis and Adalperga were the first to stir up trouble, and Adalperga easily persuaded her husband to help. They planned to incite a revolt against Charles in the former Lombard kingdom.

But scarcely had a plot begun to take shape when Charles got wind of it and sent an army marching into Italy. In the face of the armored cavalry, archers, and spear-carrying foot soldiers of the mighty Frankish armies, the proud designs of the two Lombard children crumbled at once. Frightened, Arichis sent his and Adelperga's son to Charles to plead for mercy. As proof of the honesty of his father's intentions, the young man offered to stay on at Charles's court as a hostage.

Charles, ever a father at heart, had always had a soft spot for displays of noble character in the young. Something about the courage and courtesy of this

Hands clasped on his sword, Charles observes the baptism of Widukind (d. 807), the Saxon chief whose courage was respected even by his enemies. Widukind's resourcefulness was legendary: Once, pursued by a band of armed Franks, he reversed his horse's shoes, thus sending the attackers off in the wrong direction.

grandson of Desiderius tore through the shroud of harshness that for years now had enveloped the king. A genuine fondness quickly sprung up be-

tween the two. Despite his friend Pope Hadrian's repeated urgings to attack, Charles held off. Finally he allowed Arichis's son to return home and was lenient with the Beneventans. It seemed as if Charles's generous nature had returned.

However, this was not to be the case. Desiderius's other daughter, Liutperga, and her husband, Duke Tassilo, were to taste the king's still seething, vengeful, and mistrustful spirit. Tassilo and Charles were cousins, just a year apart, and in many respects they were peers. The culture of Bavaria, Tassilo's homeland, was as ancient and rich as that of Frankland. Tassilo came from one of Bavaria's great noble families, and, like the Frankish king, he had a deep love for the church and a respect for justice that endeared him to his subjects.

In his early years Tassilo had been sincerely fond of his Frankish relatives and happy to serve them. He had sworn an oath to Charles's father, Pepin, that he would be faithful to the Frankish king and his sons all the days of his life. Yet, in later years, a more independent spirit had grown up in him, strengthened by his marriage to Liutperga. No doubt Desiderius's daughter resented seeing her husband ruled by the man who had deposed her father.

Although Charles had long tolerated this independent spirit in his cousin, it had begun to irk him in recent years. Finally, in 785, he used a minor incident as an excuse to threaten Tassilo with his massive army and to demand that he renew his old oath of allegiance. Although at his wife's urging the Duke held out for a while, eventually he gave in and complied.

But even this renewal of the oath was not enough for Charles. He was driven by the will to dominate. Sensing the reluctance in Tassilo's surrender, nothing less than complete, wholehearted submission could satisfy him.

Though previously Charles's ruthlessness surfaced as sheer physical violence, it now took the form of psychological torture. Wounding more deeply and leaving longer-lasting scars, it was this psychological punishment that Charles now employed against his cousin.

> *Subjects and enemies were astonished at his sudden presence at the moment when they believed him at the most distant extremity of the empire.*
>
> —EDWARD GIBBON

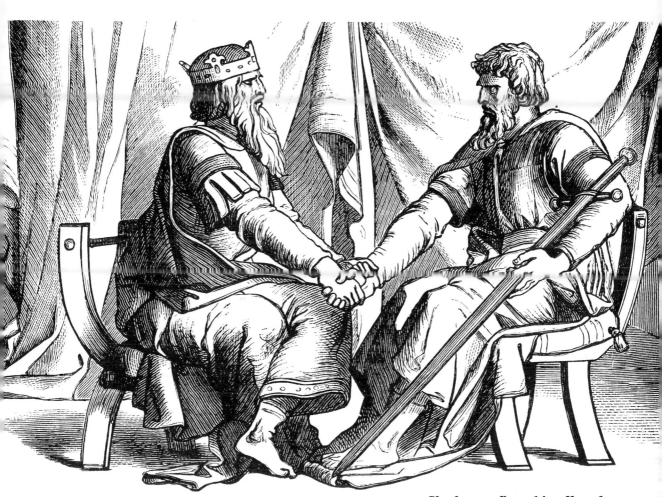

Charles confirms his offer of amnesty to Widukind after the Saxon's surrender. In 785, at Charles's request, Pope Hadrian I declared a three-day holiday throughout Christendom to honor the pagan leader's conversion to Christianity.

A year earlier, when Charles threatened Bavaria with his mighty armies, many of the Bavarian nobles had defected to the Franks. Charles now used these traitors to condemn his cousin. When Tassilo appeared at the National Assembly in 788, Charles had him seized and brought before the Frankish court. Then the procession of witnesses began.

"He plotted to kill our noble and most excellent king's emissaries."

"He said in our presence that if he had 10 sons as hostages, he would rather that all of them die than that he keep the terms of his pact."

"He said that it was better for us all to die than to live like this, in servitude."

Pope Hadrian I, Charles's longtime friend, strongly advised Duke Tassilo's nobles to refuse to support the duke's defiance of Charles's demands; afraid of incurring the pope's wrath, and intimidated by Charles's armies, the nobles not only failed to obey Tassilo but also testified against him.

Tassilo listened as in a stupor. How could they say such things? For over 30 years he had fretted over these same men's concerns, for so long he had fought for them. The truth of their words hardly mattered for it was their willingness to betray that stung. He bowed his head. Surely Charles had broken him.

Even as he pronounced Tassilo guilty of treason, Charles's conscience pricked him. He asked his cousin to name his own punishment. Tassilo, although he mistrusted this new tone of mercy, gave the expected answer: confinement to a monastery for life. Though the duke was wise to be skeptical, this new attitude heralded a thawing in the king's heart. But several years were to pass before it would become fully evident.

With Tassilo out of the way, Bavaria was easily annexed and brought under full Frankish rule. Charles now reigned over all the German peoples: Franks, Saxons, and Bavarians. His kingdom included all of present-day Belgium and Switzerland, nearly all of France, most of Germany and the Netherlands, and parts of Italy, Austria, and Yugoslavia.

Not even this achievement, however, put an end

Bavaria—which today looks much as it did when Duke Tassilo ruled it—inspired the intense loyalty of its inhabitants, who detested the thought of becoming Frankish subjects. In 788, however, Charles annexed the beautiful duchy and installed a Frankish administration.

Attila the Hun (406—453), an ancestor of the fierce Avars, was the scourge of the Roman Empire between 441 and 453. In 450 he demanded the sister of the Roman emperor as his bride, along with half the empire as a wedding present. When his request was refused, he seized northern Italy.

to fighting. Charles was as efficient an administrator as he was a conqueror. He knew he could never maintain his rule over these new eastern lands unless he could guarantee the safety of their borders.

The territory to the east of Saxony and Bavaria was the homeland of the ancestors of present-day Slavs and Hungarians. Most of these people were warlike, and they continually sparred with their Germanic neighbors.

Charles had no wish to make these people a part of Frankland, but he knew he had to force them to stop their raids across the borders. Immediately after his bloodless conquest of Bavaria, therefore,

Charles once again took to the battlefields.

These border wars, which lasted from 788 to 795, subdued most of the Slavic peoples. Terms were worked out allowing them to keep a certain amount of their independence in exchange for promises of peace and payment of tribute. The borderlands in which the king exercised partial authority were called *marches*. In addition to securing the eastern marches, during this time Charles also fought to establish marches on the Spanish border to the southwest and in Brittany to the north.

One of the later border wars, however, grew to be a major conflict east of Bavaria—the war against the Avars. The Avars were not Slavic, but Mongolian relatives of the tribe that had produced Attila the Hun three centuries earlier. Their hair, bound with ribbons, hung down their backs, and to the Franks they appeared extremely menacing. They fought with a ferocity that matched their warlike appearance. Charles knew the Avars had to be completely beaten. Halfway measures would never last. But the war turned out to be the second most costly of Charles's reign. The Avars suffered devastating losses, while many Franks lost their lives as well.

Yet the king was grandly rewarded for his efforts. The Avars' famed treasures—huge objects made entirely of gold or silver, elaborate silks, and other precious items—all fell to the Franks. It took dozens of carts to bring them back to Charles's court.

In addition to greatly enriching his kingdom, the Avar war proved to be an important turning point in Charles's reign. For nearly 15 years now, ever since the defeat at Roncesvalles, the Franks had supported their king in his relentless drive to conquer, and they had rejoiced with him in his many victories. Yet, for all their battle-pride, they had grown weary. War meant great hardships for Charles's subjects, peasant and noble alike. Since there was no standing professional army in Frankland, each time a campaign was to be waged, the king had to call upon his nobles to lead it and to supply men to fight in it. The nobles lucky enough

I am quite certain of the good will of the king, although he has fewer abettors than subverters of justice.
—ALCUIN

51

to have survived were becoming increasingly worried about the effects their continual absence was having on their estates. Harvests and plantings went unsupervised. Repairs were put off.

The common people also had cause to grumble. The life of a Frankish peasant was rough and brutal. Most were required to work three days a week on their lord's land, leaving little time to care for their own small plots. From the meager income these bits of land produced they paid numerous taxes. Now, in addition to this, for years they had been required to supply manpower, food, and equipment for the king's armies. It was too much.

The mounting discontent of these years was bound to erupt. In 785 a nobleman named Hadrad had organized a plot to murder Charles, though Charles had gotten wind of that conspiracy and quickly suppressed it. Now, in 792, whispers of treason and murder were heard again. This time a whole group of disgruntled nobles were involved in a conspiracy to depose Charles. More serious still, the nobles had persuaded one of the king's own sons—Pepin the Hunchback, whose mother was Charles's first wife—to lead the conspiracy.

At the last minute a Lombard poet who had been told about the plot warned Charles. All the conspirators were seized and sentenced to death—all, that is, except Charles's son.

Nothing was dearer to Charles than his family. He was deeply affected by the discovery that his own son was hostile toward him. Suddenly the harshness he had displayed for the past 15 years began to soften. Charles spared his son the death penalty and sent him to a monastery instead. Then, in 794, he sent for his cousin Tassilo, whom he had so cruelly treated several years earlier, and formally pardoned him.

It was too late for Tassilo to benefit from the return of gentleness in the king, for the duke's spirit had been permanently broken. But it was not too late for many others. The settlements that followed Charles's victories of the 790s were far different from the brutal terms imposed on the Saxons in the previous decade.

Let those who have only just been won to the faith be given—in the words of the Apostle Paul—milk, that is to say, gentle commandments.
—ALCUIN
English monk and scholar-in-residence
at Charles's court

Charles explains his new and lenient policies for governing the recently conquered Avar lands. Remembering the failure of his harsh, repressive treatment of the Saxons, he ordered no burdensome taxation or forcible conversion to Christianity.

This silver-plated bronze bracelet is one of the few Avar artifacts still known to exist. Most of the loot Charles took has—like the Avars themselves—disappeared. After Charles's unremitting border wars, the expression "vanished like the Avars" became a common phrase in eastern Europe.

At last the king began to see how his drive to dominate was interfering with his deep desire to win new souls for the church. He had learned that no people will willingly accept a religion that is forced upon them. So with the Avars there was no forced baptism or payment of tithes. Only those who had studied the new faith and on their own made a decision to accept it would join the church.

Even the Saxons were finally spared Charles's vengefulness. After chafing for seven years under the harsh terms of the capitulary of 785, they had once more rebelled against Frankish rule. Charles, paying the price for his earlier severity, was once more obliged to lead troops into Saxony. And again, years of bloody fighting ensued. But the events of earlier times were not to be repeated. The Saxons surrendered in 797, and when a new capitulary was drawn up, they were granted the same lenient terms the Avars had received. Charles was a changed man.

Charles reluctantly oversees the execution in 792 of the men who had planned to stage a palace revolt, depose him, and place his disinherited son, Pepin the Hunchback, on the Frankish throne. These death sentences marked the end of Charles's period of extremely harsh rule.

UNDER·A·PINE·TREE·CLOSE·TO·A·SWEET·BRIAR·ON·A·SEAT
OF·GOLD·SAT—THE·KING·OF·THE·FAIR·COUNTRY·OF·FRANCE

Charlemagne

5

Settling in at Aachen

Though there was still a nip in the air when Charles awoke, the king was quickly out of bed. He treasured these brisk, brilliant northern mornings. They were his favorite time of day.

From the minute he arose there was no rest. Stewards and counts chatted and asked advice. As he pulled on his hose and short tunic, Charles listened carefully and replied to each question. He loved to have people around him; he hardly knew what privacy meant. And he hated inefficiency. Why not hold the daily planning session in his bedroom? He scarcely needed all his energy for dressing.

Next came mass in the royal chapel, followed by the high point of the day: the morning hunt, which was one of Charles's passions. His entire family joined in the daily expeditions.

Game was plentiful in the dense northern forests, and the hunters usually returned with their kill in several hours. By this time appetites were whetted for the noon meal, for which fare was both hearty and plentiful. Charles was especially fond of roast meats, and he ate copiously. Usually the spread included fresh game roasted on a spit.

Charles regarded meals as more than an occasion to satisfy hunger. For him they were also a

Charles's octagonal chapel (center) was considered "half human, half divine," by the king's contemporaries, who also regarded it as one of the wonders of the world. In later centuries, a cathedral was built around the original structure.

Charles, who looks like a fairy-tale king in this illustration, was, in reality, very much a man of the real world. As well as governing his empire and leading its armies, he revised the currency system, established a national educational program, supervised much of Aachen's construction, and built a huge bridge across the Rhine River.

time when heart and mind were nourished. Behavior at his table was very different from the rowdy activity common at the courts of other Germanic chiefs. Only modest drinking was allowed. While eating, Charles and his family and guests listened to a reading from a book about religion or history the king had selected. Only afterward was there conversation, and then it was likely to turn to intellectual or cultural matters.

After the midday meal, Charles took a long, sound nap. He awoke refreshed and ready for whatever the rest of the day had in store. There were always legal cases to be heard, plans to be made, capitularies to be written, matters of all sort that required his study. Often he would take time out for a swim in the palace pool; the king's passion for swimming was equalled only by his love of the hunt. In fact, he frequently entertained visiting dignitaries in the pool, in the style of the ancient Roman baths. In the evening he might again attend services in the chapel.

And always there was time for his family. Charles was a doting, if domineering, father. He reveled in the company of his many children, and he involved himself intensely in every aspect of their upbringing.

From their earliest years he began to plan for the future of his sons. He kept careful watch over every aspect of their education, intent that they should prove themselves worthy of the crowns they would one day wear.

To Charles, a worthy king needed to be both civilized and hardy. Young Charles, Carloman (who was later given his half-brother's name, Pepin), and Louis received rigorous instruction from some of the finest scholars of the time. They also received extensive practical training. From the age of 10 the boys accompanied their father to battle, and by the time they were 13 they were commanding men. To give them experience in kingship, Charles had made each of his sons by Hildegarde overlord of one region of the kingdom. (Pepin the Hunchback, his son by Himiltrude, was excluded.)

Even after his sons were out on their own, Charles kept a watchful eye on them. When, for example,

> *Charles paid such attention to the upbringing of his sons and daughters that he never sat down to table without them when he was at home.*
>
> —EINHARD

Charles dreams of a visit from St. James. (Just before he invaded Spain, Charles had told of a vision in which the saint requested the liberation of his Spanish tomb from the Moslems.) Always religious, the king became even more pious as he grew older, often visiting his chapel three times a day.

Charles's simple but imposing throne, carved from a single piece of stone, dominates the interior of his chapel. The fact that the throne was positioned beneath an image of Christ in the domed ceiling was intended to remind observers that Charles ruled by divine will.

he suspected Louis of becoming a bit too frivolous in sophisticated Aquitaine, he ordered the young man to join him on the rough Saxon front.

Charles kept an even more jealous watch over his daughters. He adored the beautiful young princesses and hated to be long separated from them. The king's fondness for his daughters had a strong element of possessiveness to it. He would only let them marry courtiers living right there in the palace. He was, however, tolerant of his daughters' love affairs.

More important, the royal daughters joined in all their father's activities, from the morning hunt to the lofty after-dinner discussions the king so enjoyed. To enable them to participate in the discussions, the girls received the same schooling as their brothers.

As the years wore on and peace returned to Charles's soul, this warm home life became increasingly important to him. More and more he wearied of traveling endlessly from battlefield to battlefield. He began to long for a place to settle down. The king owned a number of palaces scattered about Frankland, but none he could truly call home.

Finally, in 791, Charles's growing urge to put down roots gave rise to one of the most magnificent building projects of the Middle Ages. He decided to build a new national capital.

As his site, Charles chose Aachen, a small town in the northern part of his realm, in what is today West Germany. Known locally for its medicinal

Accompanied by Queen Liutgard (far right) and his architect, Odo of Metz, Charles inspects the construction of his new chapel. The building's marble columns were a gift from Pope Hadrian.

springs, Aachen was within easy access of most of Frankland and was especially close to troublesome Saxony. Most important, the fact that Aachen was unknown to the world gave Charles the opportunity to make his own architectural mark, to build a great new city from its very foundations.

And Aachen did turn out to be great. The Franks were soon to acquire the great Avar treasure, and no expense had to be spared. The new city clearly bore the mark of the man who built it. A palace and a chapel formed the central unit of the new capital, a perfect symbol of the equal status of church and kingdom in Charles's mind.

Each of these structures was magnificent in its own way. The palace contained numerous special chambers—a treasure room (for storing the gold, silver, and jewels won in battle), a library, a weapons room, a wardrobe room. There was also a large marble swimming pool fed by hot springs and large enough to hold over 100 bathers.

Charles also lavished money and attention on the chapel. Inside, it was decorated with ancient mosaics from Rome (a gift from the pope), Italian marble, gold-and silver-work, and solid brass doors. The best artisans in Europe were brought to Aachen to work on it. A covered walkway connected the chapel to the palace, so that Charles and members of his family and court could attend services easily even in bad weather. Before long a bustling town had sprung up at the base of the great palace and chapel.

Charles's personal mellowing and his deepening appreciation of the quiet pleasures of his own home and court were matched by a growing desire to improve the daily lives of his subjects. Beginning in the late 780s and throughout the 790s, the king devoted more and more of his energies to managing the internal affairs of his realm. He proved himself as much a genius at these administrative tasks as he had been at battle strategy.

For years Charles had traveled through his kingdom, personally overseeing the many royal estates. Each of these estates was a nearly self-sufficient operation, producing honey, beer, wine, smoked

> *In 787 Charles was still the barbarian leader of a warrior band, a receiver and giver of gold and jewels, a victor in battle, a punisher of breach of faith ... though also the man who subjected the people of the Franks to impartial laws.*
> —DONALD BULLOUGH

Charles listens as one of his *missi dominici* (royal emissaries) reports on an inspection tour of a crown estate.
Without the *missi*, who acted as the eyes and ears of the
king, Charles would have had great difficulty in governing
his vast empire.

A silver coin minted about 804 shows Charles's head crowned by a Roman-style garland. After Charles made sound silver currency the empire's official medium of exchange, Frankish money could be used in foreign as well as domestic commerce.

Of Charlemagne's moral virtues, chastity is not the most conspicuous.

—EDWARD GIBBON

meat, cheese, mustard, cloth, shoes, and iron goods, as well as common crops and livestock. The king gave much energy to this task and soon was an expert at managing these complex enterprises.

To help his stewards, the men who ran the estates year-round, Charles circulated a document containing his recommendations for efficient management. Called the Decree Concerning the Estates, it contained many specific suggestions about how and what to grow and about how best to run each of an estate's many small industries. It also stressed such principles as being thorough and accurate in bookkeeping, maintaining proper hygiene, and keeping all tools and buildings in good repair.

Unfortunately, many of the men who oversaw the estates were lazy or corrupt. Not only did they disregard the suggestions in the decree, they often cheated the peasants who worked for them. Charles would have preferred to reprimand and reform each of these men personally, but travel was difficult and such close involvement was impossible.

Charles's ingenious solution to this dilemma was to send teams of special royal ambassadors to oversee affairs and ensure justice in the distant corners of Frankland. These ambassadors, called *missi dominici* (Latin for "the lord's emissaries"), were specially chosen for their good character. "I insist," Charles wrote, "that my *missi* are, by their upright behavior, examples of the virtues in which they instruct others in my name." He sent the *missi* out in pairs, one clergyman and one layman, with the hope that between the two of them they could handle almost any problem that might come up.

Charles also did much to improve communication and trade in his ever-growing realm. He had many new roads and bridges built, and old ones repaired. He even tried, although unsuccessfully, to build a canal connecting the great Danube and Rhine rivers. As the many different peoples of Frankland came more frequently into contact with one another, conflicts arose over the many different systems of money and weights being used. So Charles established a common system of coinage and of measurements for the realm.

Charles's concern for the well-being of his subjects went far beyond that of their physical needs, however. He also felt responsible for their minds and souls.

Charles confers with architects about foundation work on a monastery. Although the king often ordered churches and villas built of stone and brick, most buildings of his time had wooden walls and thatched roofs.

6

In Charge of Minds and Souls

For all his rough-hewn heartiness and his reputation as a man of action, Charles also cared greatly about the development of his intellect and his spirit. Ever since his exposure to the cultured ways of Italy and Aquitaine, his interest in music, languages, and theology had been as keen as his enthusiasm for the hunt. This intellectual and spiritual side of the king became more and more apparent as he settled in Aachen. He began to work as hard on his studies as he had earlier on his military campaigns. Though extremely literate, Charles wrote little of his correspondence himself. Instead, to save time, he would dictate to his clerks. He learned to speak Latin and Greek, and he helped devise a grammar of the common Germanic tongue spoken by his people. And, as in all things, Charles felt as responsible for the intellectual and spiritual well-being of his subjects as he did for his own. He never forgot his role as king.

Charles had long been dismayed by the low level of learning in his kingdom. Eager to remedy the situation, he began by establishing a school at the royal palace to which he invited students and scholars from all over his kingdom. Although this Palace

The allegorical figure of Grammar presides over the marriage of Eloquence and Learning in a book of Latin poetry that was used in the Palace School. Alcuin's texts were supplemented by copies of books whose words and illustrations had been created by Roman scholars centuries earlier.

Paying a surprise visit to the Palace School, Charles questions students about their progress in such subjects as geometry, grammar, and rhetoric. Many of the school's textbooks were the work of the monk Alcuin (735–804).

School was chiefly for the sons of nobles, Charles believed that all would benefit from a good education. In fact, he liked to point out that in the classroom the poorer boys often far outshone the spoiled sons of the nobility. Charles even approved of educated women, a very unusual attitude for a man of his time. He dreamed of one day being able to offer free education to all in his kingdom.

The reputation of the Palace School quickly spread. Soon it was attracting the keenest minds from all over Europe. Charles stood in awe of many of his new scholarly guests, but one in particular attracted his attention. This was a quiet monk from England named Alcuin.

The king soon recognized that although Alcuin did not have a very original mind, he had the makings of a great teacher. Charles quickly offered Alcuin handsome terms to come live at the palace and take charge of his programs of education. Under the English monk's able direction, Charles's dream of raising the educational level of his people began to become a reality.

Alcuin wrote new textbooks to replace the error-riddled ones used by the Franks in the past. He used the Palace School to train teachers, and set about establishing a grammar school at each of the many abbeys in Frankland. The abbeys, residences and places of worship for monks, were also centers of learning and art. By the time Alcuin retired, 15 years after he had come to Aachen, Charles was able to propose universal free education to his subjects. This was a first in the history of the world. Not even the great Roman emperors could boast such an achievement.

Charles also took great personal delight in Alcuin's presence at the palace. His own interests were wide-ranging, and he relished the new after-dinner talk that had developed now that Alcuin and other scholars were regulars at his table. For hours, conversation alternated from questions of theology to principles of astronomy.

These gatherings of the intellectually minded members of the court soon became a formal institution at Aachen. Participants referred to them-

We permit anyone who wishes, for the love of God and his saints, to set up images inside or outside the churches, but we shall never force anyone to worship them, nor allow any others to destroy them.
—CHARLES
in the Caroline Books, a treatise written by Charles for the Council of Frankfurt defending the Western church's position on idolatry

Charles listens to a Palace School pupil demonstrate his skill in Latin composition. Far more interested in academic excellence than social backgrounds, the king did not discriminate between rich and poor students.

Charles dictates a capitulary, or series of laws, to Alcuin, whose many duties included those of scribe. Although Charles considered the scholarly monk an indispensable aide, he finally permitted him to retire, appointing him abbot of the monastery of St. Martin of Tours, one of the wealthiest religious institutions in the Frankish Empire.

selves as "the Academy." They met informally but frequently, to hear lectures, share poems they had written, discuss the burning issues of the day, or even challenge themselves with riddles.

It was perhaps at these meetings of the Academy that Charles was most endearing. Uninhibited by any pride of rank, he was not at all shy of admitting where he was ignorant or possibly wrong. He had the insatiable, lively curiosity of a schoolboy.

The members of the Academy gave each other nicknames. Charles himself was dubbed "King David." This nickname was an especially apt one, for David's role in the Bible is that of a prophet-king, and Charles, now in his 50s, viewed himself in the same way.

His great concern with education sprang largely from concern for his people's moral and spiritual

> *Charles knew that a kingdom is like a body and is agitated now by this and now by that trouble if it is not cared for by good advice and strength as doctors keep a body in health.*
> —anonymous biographer of Louis the Pious

Alcuin, the English monk who made Charles's dream of public education a reality, also served his king as close friend, tutor, religious authority, and political advisor.

well-being. Education was valuable chiefly because it opened a person to the religious knowledge that made for salvation of the soul. One of the chief aims of the schools that Charles founded was to educate more men to make copies of the Bible.

Charles became involved in the religious life of Frankland in other ways as well. In earlier years his sense of religious mission had been confined to his attempts to gain new converts from his exploits on the battlefield. He had been content to leave the nourishing of Christian souls to the church. Now, his sense of his spiritual responsibility for his subjects began to expand.

The king spent much energy trying to reform the Frankish church. Above all, he was concerned that people, and especially the clergy, should live up to the ideals of behavior they professed. The king often turned preacher, and gave stern public sermons against vice and impiety.

Charles also worked hard to make the church services in Frankland beautiful and dignified. In the years before his reign people had grown accustomed to using the churches as storage barns, littering them with hay and tools. Services went on amidst the clutter, bumbled through by uneducated priests who used broken Latin, interrupted by the chatter of parishioners. Charles brought an end to such scenes. He undertook to see that all the churches in his realm were repaired and cleaned. He introduced the beautiful Gregorian chant to the church services. And he urged priests to get a proper education.

In his new role as defender of the faith, Charles also began to get involved in the raging theological controversies of the day. He took these questions seriously, had them studied at court, and did all he could to see that the orthodox position, that is, the one that accorded most closely with church tradition, won out. He also began to step in when he felt that his old friend Pope Hadrian was slacking off at his duties in these areas.

The most important controversy of Charles's time centered around the question of what role images should play in Christian worship. For many years

[Charles's] own studies were tardy, laborious, and imperfect ... but the curiosity of the human mind must ultimately tend to its improvement.

—EDWARD GIBBON

Most of the books used in Charles and Alcuin's schools were, like the volume containing this portrait of a saintly scribe, about religious matters. Because literary style was highly regarded, however, pagan classical writers were also studied.

A monk of Charles's era copies a manuscript onto parchment. This heavy paper, which was made from sheepskin, was expensive, and the monks often "washed" older manuscripts in order to reuse their paper for books they considered more important. Aided by infrared techniques, modern scholars can sometimes uncover the original texts.

Eastern Christians had relied heavily on images of Jesus, Mary, and the saints in their spiritual life, and in 787 the emperor in Constantinople, Constantine VI, gave a formal defense of this practice.

When Charles heard the words of the defense, he sensed heresy afoot. (Heresy is any belief that is opposed to official doctrine.) Images could help in the building of faith and in instruction, the Western Church maintained, but should not themselves be worshiped. Charles notified Pope Hadrian of the danger he sensed in the East's emphasis on images. He urged him to take action.

Hadrian wrote Charles a warm letter in reply, but did nothing. Then, inspired by "love of God and a taste for the truth," Charles decided to take the matter into his own hands. He composed a long and vigorous defense of the Western Church's position and in 794 called a great council of bishops in the city of Frankfurt, where he had it read.

The council was easily persuaded by the eloquent and tightly argued prose of what are now called the Caroline Books. Charles had shown that he could even hold his own against learned theologians. Those present voted to approve Charles's request for a condemnation of the Eastern position. Even the representatives of the pope were won over, but Hadrian's respect for the king was strong and he allowed Charles's ruling to stand.

Throughout their long friendship—it had been almost 20 years since they had first met—Hadrian and Charles had repeatedly made plays for power traditionally held by the other. Each had had his turn at bowing to the other's greater strength. Hadrian had blocked Charles from assuming political power in Rome, even though this had been officially granted the Franks when they drove out the Lombards. Charles had refused the pope's repeated requests for more land.

Yet, despite the storms and struggles, their friendship was a steady one. A certain equality between the great warrior king and the illustrious pope, cemented by their common devotion to the church and their deep affection for each other, had maintained a balance of power.

> Whoever stole you from that bush of broom, / I think he envied me my happiness, / O little nightingale, for many a time / You lightened my sad heart from its distress, / And flooded my whole soul with melody.
> —ALCUIN

Some of the religious books in Charles's library were bound with intricately carved ivory covers like this one, which shows the crucifixion. The work of monks, these bindings were much treasured by the king, despite the fact that they were frequently influenced by the imagery of the Eastern church, which Charles considered heretical.

In 795, just a year after the meeting in Frankfurt, Pope Hadrian died. When he heard the news, Charles wept. He was deeply grieved by the passing of his loyal and noble-hearted friend.

Though he could not know it at the time, Charles had lost more than a friend. With Hadrian's passing, the delicate balance between king and pope, between Aachen and Rome, had also ended.

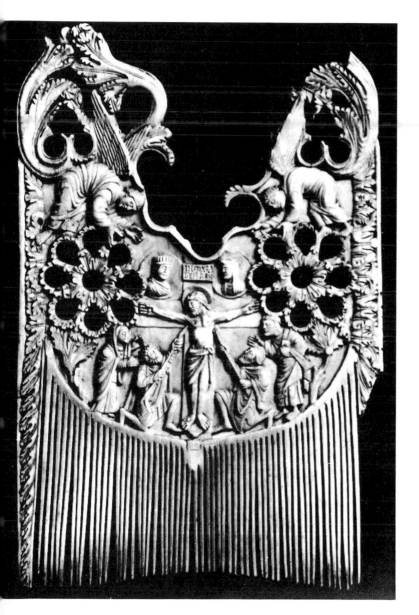

Known as "St. Heribert's comb," this magnificent example of medieval ivory carving—an art that reached its highest point during Charles's reign—depicts angels sorrowfully watching the crucifixion of Christ. The flower-like designs represent the tree of life, an often-used theme in the sacred art of eastern Christendom.

7
The Road to Empire

In the year 800 the ancient splendor that had been Rome was more than just a memory. It had not been long in terms of history—only a few hundred years—since the Western Roman Empire had fallen.

Rome's grand old buildings still stood proudly, marred by years of poor upkeep, but not as yet destroyed. The famous Colosseum, a huge outdoor arena built in the first century, was still in use. The same aristocratic families that had governed the city in the time of the Caesars still had great power. The language of Rome's citizens was still commonly spoken throughout Europe.

Charles had long been drawn to this great city, attracted by its culture, its noble past, and by the power that seemed a part of its very air. Yet, at the same time he was distrustful of Rome. The vigorous Frankish king appreciated civilization, but to him Rome's civilized ways bordered on decadence. He barred his sons from visiting the city during their impressionable early years. And Charles himself insisted on remaining garbed in his humble Frankish outfit while visiting there.

With Hadrian's death, however, everything changed. Charles was soon to be drawn more deeply

In 799 King Charles was head of the world, a man to be acclaimed as the crowning glory of Europe, father of the continent, Augustus; a sovereign with his own capital, a 'second Rome,' worthily provided with buildings; the monarch to whom the chief bishop of the world turned for protection and help.
—DONALD BULLOUGH

The Holy Roman Empire's golden crown, placed on Charles's head by Pope Leo, is studded with emeralds and sapphires and topped with a jeweled cross and an arch carrying the name of an earlier Roman emperor. The crown is preserved today in an Austrian museum.

A 19th-century engraving of Charles shows him as a blond, Teutonic hero. No undisputed portrait of Charles exists, but a chronicler of the period noted that the king's height measured "seven times his own foot"—making him at least a head taller than most Franks.

into Roman affairs, with consequences he could but dimly discern.

The man who followed Hadrian on the throne of Saint Peter was nothing like the popular patrician (a member of one of the original aristocratic families of ancient Rome) who had just died. Pope Leo III, a Roman of humble birth, was resented by the Roman aristocracy, some of whom accused him of immorality. Leo sensed that to survive he would have to have protection, and this proved to be true.

One morning in the spring of 799, on his way to the church of St. Lawrence, the pope was attacked by a group of conspirators who were determined to depose him. They rushed towards his horse, grabbed the Pope's flowing robes, and pulled him to the ground. When he awoke, Leo found himself in the prison cell of a monastery. His robes were gone, his body covered with bruises and cuts. From here the conspirators took him to a convent, from which he was finally rescued by loyal attendants. Immediately he sought refuge with Frankish ambassadors.

Charles himself was not fond of the new pope. Leo's character did not stand up in comparison with Hadrian's, and Charles could not help comparing. The king suspected that the Roman nobles' charges of adultery against the new pope might even be true. Nevertheless, Charles's deeply pious nature was outraged at the news of the brutal treatment of Leo. Whatever one's personal feelings about a pope, such an assault on the man who was the head of the church was inexcusable. Charles ordered his representatives in Rome to send Leo to him at once.

Leo stayed with Charles at Paderborn for several months. No one knows what the two men talked about during that long Saxon summer, but by fall Charles was convinced that he ought to do all in his power to see the pope restored to his throne.

In November 799 the king sent Leo back to Rome accompanied by Frankish bodyguards and two archbishops, who were to conduct an investigation that would clear the pope's name. He also gave Leo a fatherly warning to be on his best behavior. Yet this was not to be the end of the affair. Forces had

Generous of hand, gentle of soul, and mild of speech, doing good to all and working harm to none, she studiously pursues the liberal arts.
—THEODULF OF ORLEANS
Frankish chronicler, describing
Liutgard, Charles's fifth wife.

been unleashed in the summer at Paderborn that had only begun to spin themselves out.

The spring following Leo's return to Rome, Charles set off on a tour of his kingdom, the most thorough he had made in years. He visited even the most distant marches, checking at every stop to be sure that Frankish overlordship was secure. En route he made a number of stops at shrines, where he prayed and consulted with his most trusted advisers. But what was on Charles's mind during these months remains a mystery.

The tour had an unhappy ending for the king. On its last leg, his beautiful and charming fifth wife, Liutgard, fell ill and died. Charles was dispirited; he had greatly loved this woman who had brought grace and serenity to his new, more settled life. But he did not allow himself to linger long in his mourning, as he might have done in earlier years. A new soberness and determination had taken hold of him.

Late in that summer of 800 Charles announced

An artist's reconstruction of the city of Rome as it probably appeared during the time of the dictator Julius Caesar (100 B.C.–44 B.C.), who died eight centuries before Charles was born. Although partially destroyed by invading barbarians in 455, the city still possessed much of its ancient grandeur when Charles saw it.

that he was going to Rome. He wanted to have his oldest legitimate son, Charles, officially anointed as king of the Franks. (It was customary for Frankish heirs to be crowned before their predecessors died.) Also, the investigation into the pope's alleged improprieties had bogged down, and Charles thought his help was needed to clear Leo.

The king's reception in Rome was that of a hero. Huge crowds lined the streets, cheering and waving standards. For centuries Romans had been too proud and suspicious to accept the rule of outsiders with anything but a grudging spirit. But there was something about the tall Frankish warrior that won them over.

To begin with, the Romans were grateful to Charles. In 774 he had freed them from the hated Lombards. He had also showered them with gifts. More important, he was someone who could inspire them as had the caesars in days gone by. Their present pope could not play such a role; the

The present St. Peter's, completed in 1626, occupies the site of the basilica where Charles was crowned emperor in 800. Although the original church, built over the tomb of St. Peter in the fourth century, was severely damaged by repeated barbarian attacks, the tomb—which is still in place—remained untouched.

king of the Franks was now the only one who could stir enthusiasm.

The stalled investigation of the pope was cleared up in less than a month. Leo swore a solemn oath declaring his innocence. Charles then turned his attention to preparations for his son's anointing, and a Christmas Day ceremony in St. Peter's Cathedral was planned.

On the morning of December 25, 800, Charles entered the packed nave (central hall) of St. Peter's. Throngs of people representing all the lands he ruled and had relations with had come to Rome for the event. In the glowing light of hundreds of candles, the king could make out the costumes of Romans, Franks, Bavarians, Lombards, even of Anglo-Saxons and Greeks. Charles himself, in a rare concession to the citizens of Rome, had dressed in the long tunic, cloak, and sandals of a Roman nobleman.

The king walked slowly down the long aisle to

Holding a document that lists accusations against the pope, Charles greets Leo III (d. 816) at Paderborn in 799. The king had strong doubts about Leo's personal integrity, but he nevertheless remained a loyal supporter of the papacy.

the front row where his children were seated. His face was solemn, composed, his thoughts hidden.

Once at the altar, Charles knelt in prayer. It was a long time before he arose, but when he did his eyes caught sight of the crowns. There on the altar sat not one gold crown, but two.

Pope Leo reached for the larger of the crowns and placed it on the king's grizzled head. At once a great cry began to fill the church. "Long life and victory to Charles Augustus, crowned by God, great

A wall mosaic in Rome's church of St. John Lateran shows St. Peter bestowing the papal stole—symbol of spiritual leadership—on Leo III (left), and the imperial banner—the symbol of worldly power—on King Charles. The words of the Latin inscription mean: "Blessed Peter, give long life to Pope Leo and victory to King Charles."

Accompanied by trumpeters, standard bearers, and soldiers, Charles passes through a Frankish village during a tour of inspection in 800.

and peaceful emperor of the Romans," the crowd roared. Three times they repeated it.

The repetition of this chant had its origins in the ancient ceremony by which a man became emperor of the Romans. Rome had not had an emperor of her own since the assassination of the Emperor Orestes in 476 more than 300 years earlier, but she had one now—the king of the Franks.

To this day, no one is sure if Charles knew beforehand that this was to take place. He remained regal and composed as Leo continued with the ceremony and crowned his son. Yet, Einhard, Charles's

Charles receives petitioners in his throne room at Aachen. One of the important officials of the court was the chief doorkeeper. Like a modern appointments secretary, the doorkeeper made the decisions about who would—or would not—be admitted to the king's presence.

biographer and one of his closest friends, remembered the king saying that he would never have entered St. Peter's that Christmas Day if he had known what the pope was planning to do.

We can never know if this remark of Charles's was meant literally. Still, it is important for what it shows about the new emperor's attitude. Whether or not Charles had taken a part in the planning for this new role, he accepted it in a spirit of humility, almost of reluctant duty. Certainly this was the chance of which he had dreamed for many years. It was an opportunity, with the blessing of the pope himself, to apply his many talents to the task of making Christendom a true kingdom of God on earth. Yet, now that the dream was about to become a reality, Charles could see that so immense a job was almost too much for one man, even a man as extraordinarily capable as himself.

Pope Leo solemnly crowns the kneeling Charles on Christmas Day, 800. His full title thereafter was: "Charles, Most Serene Augustus, crowned by God, great and peaceful Emperor, governing the Roman Empire, and by the mercy of God, king of the Lombards and the Franks."

8

Charles the Great

In July 802 all of Aachen had lined the streets to greet the new arrival. It had not been long since the last time they had turned out in this way. On the previous occasion they had strained their necks to get a glimpse of the tall, regal form of the newly crowned emperor returning home mounted high astride his horse. This time they were looking for something even more astounding

At last a large gray shape appeared on the horizon and an excited murmur swept through the crowd. Could this be it—the strange, giant beast of which they had heard so many stories?

It was. The caliph of Baghdad, leader of the Moslems, had sent Charles a very unusual gift —an elephant named Abul Abbas. At this time very few Europeans had ever seen an elephant. Now one of the great mammals was to be a household pet at the palace. Abul Abbas quickly became a great favorite in Aachen. The court loved to watch him swish his trunk. The emperor grew so attached to him that he took him along on all his expeditions as if he were the family dog.

During his reign as emperor, Charles tried to blend the best of two worlds: the grandeur and splendor of the old Roman Empire and the simple,

In 802 Frankish courtiers and commoners alike were astounded by the breathtaking array of valuable gifts sent to Charles by the caliph of Baghdad. Most impressive of all was Abul Abbas, the elephant that became the beloved pet of the king.

This jeweled sculpture appears on a 13th-century reliquary made to hold some of Charles's bones. When the king's tomb was opened in the year 1000, an amulet resembling the one he wears here was found at his neck; it was said to contain hairs from the head of the Virgin Mary.

hardy life of a devout German kingdom. Like the emperor's pet elephant, who died after eight years of harsh northern winters, Charles's empire was a truly wondrous thing, but one that could not last.

After the crowning, Charles stayed on in Rome for several months, working to lay the groundwork for this new empire. He gave his all to the task before him, and spent long hours studying books on the history of the ancient emperors.

Charles found much inspiration in the stories of the great emperors of old. Yet he was too much his own man to ignore his own ways and suddenly become a latter-day caesar. He retained his simple habits and plain costume, and chided those of his courtiers who rushed to adopt the refined ways of Rome. He preferred to be addressed as "king of the Franks," rather than as "emperor." He reassured his people that he would not move the capital to Rome and returned to Aachen in 801.

Charles saw his new role as fundamentally different from that of the ancient emperors. His devoutness and his sense of mission had deepened in recent years, and he now saw himself above all as a *Christian* emperor. The new imperial coins he had minted had his picture on one side, and a cross and the words "Christiana Religio" on the other.

How did Charles see the role of a "Christian emperor"? Even as king of the Franks he had thought of himself as a defender of the church. Now he saw his responsibilities to his fellow Christians as being even greater. Although he still acknowledged the pope's supreme authority, he began to see himself as very nearly the church's earthly head. Charles's concern now reached to the farthest corners of Christendom.

The Middle East in particular commanded his attention. Ever since Christ's death, the Holy Land had been a special place for Christians. Numerous monasteries had been built there and many Christians made pilgrimages, or religious journeys, to the area. But recently, reports had reached Europe of Moslem attacks on Christian monasteries in the Holy Land.

In order to ensure the safety of Christians, Charles

> *Charles was the greatest and most distinguished of men.*
> —EINHARD

**Emissaries from Harun al-Rashid deliver their leader's re-
spects to Charles in 802. Eager to secure Harun's protection of Christians in the Holy Land, Charles had made
special efforts to be friendly with the Moslem leader, who
reciprocated by honoring his new friend's wishes.**

A robe and sandal worn by Charles. Although he wore Roman-style garments when he was in Rome, and magnificent costumes for ceremonial occasions, Charles was uncomfortable with the trappings of royalty. He preferred simple clothing and an unpretentious life style.

began vigorous efforts—such as sending a team of ambassadors to Baghdad—to befriend the Moslems. His efforts were rewarded. Harun al-Rashid, the caliph of Baghdad, showered the emperor with samples of the great riches of the Islamic lands— splendid embroidered silks, a multi-storied tent, and of course the famous elephant. What was even more important was that Christians enjoyed for most of Charles's reign years of peace in the often turbulent Middle East.

As emperor, Charles was interested in peace rather than in conquest. He devoted much energy to such tasks as writing down and clarifying the laws of the many different peoples he ruled, so that these could be more fairly interpreted. In only one instance did Charles's old harshness show itself.

Saxon chronicles of the first decades of the ninth century tell one tale of misery after another. They are filled with stories of men stripped of all possessions, women and children separated from husbands and fathers, people struggling to survive in a strange and hostile land. The roots of such misery can be directly traced to the king of the Franks and emperor of the Romans. In 804 the Saxons had again rebelled, and Charles had decided to put an end to what he viewed as a chronic menace. He ordered great masses of Saxons to be removed from their homeland and transported to distant parts of the Frankish kingdom. The suffering this caused to thousands of people was severe indeed, but this was the last vestige of Charles's ruthless streak. For the most part, the fighting that took place after

A modern map of the Middle East. The city of Baghdad (now the capital of Iraq) still enjoys much of the prominence in the Moslem world that it possessed in Charles's time. The Holy Land, Christ's birthplace, is part of what is now Israel.

Charles's crowning consisted of border wars whose chief aims were defense and protection of the realm.

His main enemy in these years were the Greeks, also called Byzantines. For centuries emperors who could trace their ancestry back to the ancient emperors of Rome had sat on the throne in the Byzantine capital of Constantinople. Since the end of the Western Roman Empire, in 476, these Eastern emperors had considered themselves the rightful inheritors of the title "Roman emperor" and of the power that went along with it. They controlled much of southern Italy and were angered by Charles's domination of the Italian lands they felt were technically theirs. Now the bold northern king had the audacity to call himself emperor of the Romans as well. This was too much for the Byzantines. Tension began to mount.

The year 805 marked the beginning of a long struggle for control of Venice, a city that had traditionally been loyal to the Byzantines. In the interest of restoring friendly relations, Charles eventually ceded Venice to the emperor in Constantinople.

Meanwhile, two new enemies had appeared on the scene. The first were bands of North African Arabs who had taken up piracy, frequently raiding the lands that bordered the Mediterranean. A second group also threatened the Frankish empire from the sea. These were the inhabitants of what is now Denmark, who were known then as the Northmen, or Normans. The Northmen were famous for their fine boats, and recently they had begun to use them to conduct fierce raids on the coastal villages of Frankland.

Charles was especially alarmed by the northern raids. The Northmen were among the fiercest fighters he had yet encountered, and many of their attacks occurred at sea, where the land-loving Franks were weakest. Charles, ever resourceful, immediately set about organizing his people to build a navy. By the last years of his reign peace had returned to the north. But it was a fragile truce owing more to the death of the Danish king, Godfred, than to the strength of the Franks. The limits of Charles's powers were beginning to show.

No war ever undertaken by the Frankish people was more prolonged, more full of atrocities or more demanding of effort.

—EINHARD
on the many conflicts between the Franks and the Saxons

The 10th-century artist who made this copy of an earlier drawing of Charles gave him a drooping mustache and a slightly Oriental look. The copyist apparently forgot to include the orb that was traditionally portrayed resting in the king's right hand.

In 810 the Franks set out on a campaign against the Northmen, and Charles took his cherished companion Abul Abbas with him. Without warning the elephant suddenly died. Abul Abbas was mourned as though he had been a member of the family. In fact, not long before, Charles had lost his sister Gisla, to whom he had been deeply devoted all his life. It began to seem as if a curse had suddenly fallen on the emperor's family.

As the fateful year of 810 wore on, the bad news multiplied. The Frankish empire was swept by a mysterious cattle plague. Then, more personal tragedy: Death came for both Charles's favorite daughter, Hrodrud, and his son Pepin.

The string of deaths plunged the emperor into a mood of deep despair. While Charles had enjoyed extraordinarily good health all his life, now even it began to fail. He began to limp, to have trouble sleeping. He could no longer easily digest the roast meats that he loved (although he still insisted on trying, to his doctors' dismay). One day Charles, the master horseman, was badly thrown by his

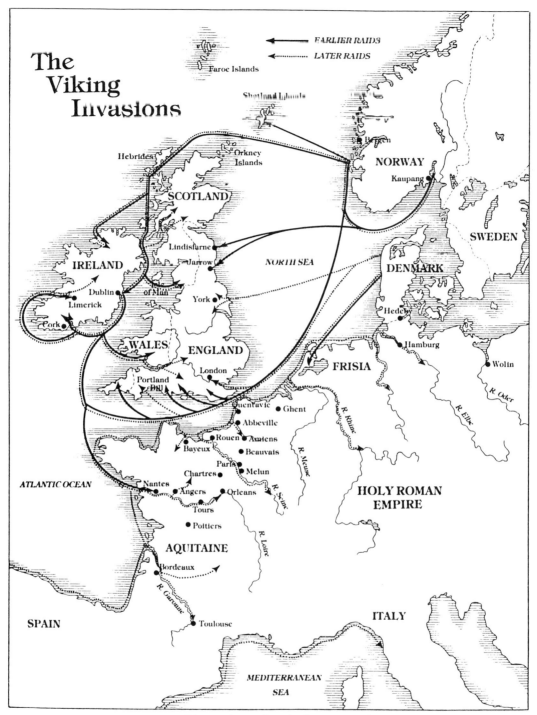

The Viking Invasions

EARLIER RAIDS
LATER RAIDS

Faroe Islands

Shetland Islands

Bergen

NORWAY

Kaupang

SWEDEN

Hebrides

Orkney
Islands

SCOTLAND

DENMARK

IRELAND

Lindisfarne

Jarrow

NORTH SEA

Hedeby

Dublin

of Man

York

Limerick

Cork

WALES

ENGLAND

Hamburg

Wolin

London

FRISIA

R. Oder

Portland
Bill

R. Elbe

Quentavic

Ghent

R. Rhine

Abbeville

ATLANTIC OCEAN

Rouen

Amiens

Bayeux

Beauvais

R. Meuse

Chartres

Paris

Melun

Nantes

Angers

Orleans

R. Seine

HOLY ROMAN
EMPIRE

Tours

Poitiers

R. Loire

AQUITAINE

Bordeaux

R. Garonne

ITALY

SPAIN

Toulouse

MEDITERRANEAN
SEA

Throughout the ninth century, bands of fierce, piratical Vikings, or Northmen, sailed out from the Scandinavian countries to wage countless raids, ravaging coastal towns in both Frankland and the British Isles.

mount. This was so rare an occurrence that his friends were alarmed.

Thoughts of his own approaching end were not new to Charles. Several years earlier he had made elaborate preparations for passing on the empire to his sons. Then, still vigorous, his chief concern had been to preserve peace. The Frankish custom that insisted a father divide up his inheritance among all his sons often made for bitter rivalries between brothers. Many innocent people could be drawn into the turmoil if the brothers involved were kings. Charles worked hard to prevent this custom of partition from destroying peace for his subjects. In the document laying out terms for the empire's division, he insisted that the three sub-kingdoms cooperate with each other.

Now, in 811, Charles began to contemplate death in more spiritual terms. More and more, his thoughts turned to the state of his soul. Charles had an active conscience, and he could no longer repress its insistent voice. Despite his mellowing in the past decade, memories of past cruelties haunted him. He keenly felt the need to make amends.

Shiploads of Northmen, with shields hung from the rails of their warships, sail to attack a Frankish shoreline settlement. The success of the Northmen's raids was largely due to the mobility of their fleets, which enabled them to land, loot, and leave before the local defenders could be mobilized.

Charles, weary and mournful, watches an advancing convoy of Norse ships, their prows carved into snarling dragon's heads. Although the Frankish military lost few battles on land, they were ill-trained for warfare at sea, the specialty of the relentless and terrifying Northmen.

He drew up a will whose chief purpose was to ensure that the vast bulk of his great treasure—a full eleven-twelfths—would go to the church. And in the will he spelled out in detail how his property was to be divided up.

At this time the emperor also began devoting much of his waning energy to writing sermons. These long tracts, which urged his people to be humble and to abide by the laws of the church, were read across the realm in public squares. Affairs of state no longer engrossed him. The once-worldly king thought seriously of renouncing the throne and becoming a monk or a pilgrim.

The final blow came in 811. Charles's oldest son and namesake, Charles, died mysteriously. This was the third child he had lost in a little over a year, and this was the child of whom the emperor was especially fond, the young man whom everyone acknowledged had all his father's extraordinary qualities.

Now only one son remained to whom Charles could pass on the great empire he had built. That was Louis, the one of all his sons who seemed lacking in the courage and forceful character that were the hallmarks of the men in the royal family. So serious were Louis's deficiencies that many at court felt the laws of succession should be waived and the crown passed to one of Charles's grandsons instead.

Charles, deeply conservative at heart, insisted on abiding by tradition. Despite his own reservations, he believed God must have some reason for wanting Louis to be emperor. Yet Charles was not a fatalist. With the time and energy that still remained he felt obliged to groom his wayward son for the awesome responsibilities that would soon fall on him.

In the summer of 813 he summoned Louis to Aachen, and there kept him close by his side for several months. Charles's fatherly advice seemed to have had little impact in the past. As ruler of Aquitaine, Louis had needed repeated counseling by the royal court. Nevertheless, Charles once again busied himself with efforts to impart his great store

> *[Charles] never withdrew from an enterprise which he had once begun and was determined to see through to the end, simply because of the labor involved.*
> —EDWARD GIBBON

of wisdom about ruling and dealing with men.

In September the succession became official. Courtiers and churchmen packed the cathedral at Aachen for what they sensed might be one of their emperor's last great public events. The crowd sat in reverent silence as the familiar though stooped figure, leaning heavily on his son's arm, slowly approached the altar and knelt in prayer. Then, as if he were again a strong warrior 30 years of age, Charles released Louis's arm, rose, and faced his people.

The words were addressed to Louis, but they seemed to be meant for all time. His exhortations to love and fear God, to defend the church, to be kind to all his family, and to treat his people as his sons seemed as much a summing up of his own reign and of the ideals that had inspired it as they did directives to his son.

Charles spoke for a long time. His energy once again seemed inexhaustible. At last he took the gleaming gold crown from the altar and himself placed it on Louis's head. There was no need now of priest or pope. The authority of Charles the Great, king of the Franks, emperor of the Romans, and leader of all Christendom, would suffice.

The crowning of Louis was one of Charles's greatest moments, the culmination of a 45-year reign unique in the history of Europe. Seldom had one man wielded so much power, both worldly and spiritual, nor made so much of what was entrusted to him. But the brilliant light brought into the world by the rule of this great king was not destined to shine much longer.

Just months after Louis was crowned, Charles returned from a hunting trip in the forests near Aachen feeling feverish and sick. By February of 814 he was dead at the age of 71.

The death of the beloved king and emperor was mourned throughout Europe. Memories of Charles soon swelled to the rank of legend. Even while he lived, people had begun to refer to him as "Charles the Great," or, in the new French language that was then emerging, as "Charlemagne." Soon stories of the king and emperor represented him in

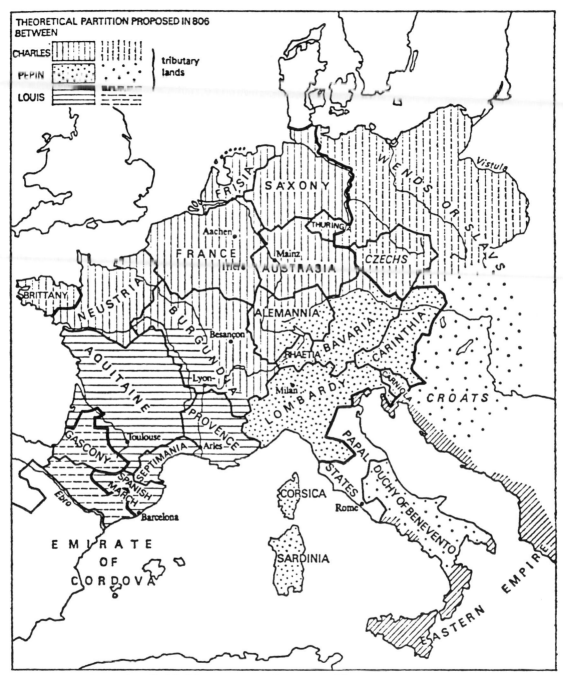

THEORETICAL PARTITION PROPOSED IN 806 BETWEEN

CHARLES
PEPIN
LOUIS

tributary lands

Vistula

FRISIA
SAXONY
WENDS OR SLAVS
THURINGIA
Aachen
FRANCE
Mainz
AUSTRASIA
Trier
CZECHS
BRITTANY
NEUSTRIA
BURGUNDY
ALEMANNIA
BAVARIA
CARINTHIA
CROATS
Besançon
RHAETIA
Lyon
CARNIOLA
AQUITAINE
Milan
LOMBARDY
PROVENCE
GASCONY
Toulouse
SEPTIMANIA
Arles
SPANISH MARCH
PAPAL STATES
DUCHY OF BENEVENTO
Ebro
CORSICA
Barcelona
Rome
EMIRATE OF CORDOVA
SARDINIA
EASTERN EMPIRE

Charles had planned to divide his mighty empire among his sons; Charles (d. 811), Pepin (d. 810), and Louis (778–840). However, due to the early deaths of the two older heirs, Louis, the least capable of the royal brothers, inherited the entire realm.

In this dual portrait, Louis (left) and Charles wear matching crowns. Charles worked hard to train his son in the arts of kingship, but Louis remained weak, impulsive, and indecisive. His ineffectual, 27-year reign marked the beginning of the end for the empire that Charles had built.

near saintly terms. For centuries to come, Charles's life would be an inspiration for others who aspired to greatness in their roles as heads of state.

The fate of the empire, however, was not nearly so glorious as that of the man who had built it. Great as it was, the structure Charles had created was inseparable from the man who had brought it into being. Therein lay its downfall. Despite Charles's consultations with advisers, his regular discussions with the councils of nobles, and his use of the *missi dominici*, the empire had been run by one man. Only someone with his own immense energy and strength of character could hold it together.

Louis could not begin to fill his father's shoes, nor could Charles's grandsons. Within two generations Charles's worst fears had been realized. The empire had been divided by bitter struggles between royal brothers and between kings and their nobles. Weakened internally, the Franks soon fell prey to the menacing Northmen and slipped back into an age nearly as dark as the one they had known a century earlier. The true flowering of medieval Europe would not come for several hundred years, and then it would be due, not to one great man, but to new structures of trade and communication that had grown up across the continent.

Charlemagne's dream of a Christian Europe, politically united under a single enlightened ruler, began to fade with his own death. But his dream did not end in failure. Charlemagne's legacy to the future—his conviction that the best elements of many cultures could be blended to produce a superior civilization—lived on.

Charlemagne's rule occurred during the centuries that would come to be known, because of their sharp decline in education, science, and the arts, as the Dark Ages. But out of that long night of barbarism, his reign gleams like a bright torch. His support for learning, science, and literature; his efforts to make the church a powerful force for unity and scholarship; his consolidation of the laws and practices of the different cultures within his

Louis, Charles's third son and only successor, was known as "the Pious" because of his religious zeal and his deep respect for the papacy. This contemporary portrait illustrated a poem written in his honor; the words can be read down or across, like a crossword puzzle.

kingdom—all these left an indelible mark on the generations that succeeded him. As long as there

are records of human history, the name of Charlemagne—Charles the Great—will endure.

Surrounded by priests and monks, Charles receives the final sacraments. Following his usual practice, he had tried to cure his final fever by fasting, but pleurisy overcame him within a week. According to his biographer, his last words were: "Into thy hands, O Lord, I commend my spirit."

The sons of Louis the Pious, Lothar (d. 855), Louis the German (d. 876), and Charles the Bald (d. 877), sign the Peace of Verdun in 843. This pact divided the Holy Roman Empire into three parts and led to its ultimate disintegration. Constant battles among Charles's descendants left his realm vulnerable to destructive invasions, particularly from the Northmen.

Further Reading

Boussard, Jacques. *The Civilization of Charlemagne*, tr. Frances Partridge. New York and Toronto: McGraw-Hill, 1979.

Bullough, Donald A. *The Age of Charlemagne.* New York: Putnam, 1966.

Easton, Stewart C. and Helene Wieruszowski. *The Era of Charlemagne.* New York: D. Van Nostrand, 1961.

Einhard and Notker the Stammerer. *Two Lives of Charlemagne*, tr. Lewis Thorpe. New York: Penguin Books, 1969.

Folz, Robert. *The Coronation of Charlemagne: 25 December 800*, tr. J.E. Anderson. London: Routledge and Kegan Paul, 1974.

Heer, Friedrich. *Charlemagne and His World.* London: Weidenfeld and Nicolson, 1975.

Lamb, Harold. *Charlemagne: the Legend and the Man.* New York: Doubleday, 1954.

Munz, Peter. *The Origin of the Carolingian Empire.* Atlantic Highlands, New Jersey: Humanities Press, 1960.

Pirenne, Henri. *Mohammed and Charlemagne.* New York: Barnes and Noble, 1968.

Riche, Pierre. *Daily Life in the World of Charlemagne*, tr. Jo Ann McNamara. Philadelphia, Pennsylvania: University of Pennsylvania Press, 1978.

Sullivan, Richard E. *Aix-la-Chapelle in the Age of Charlemagne.* Norman, Oklahoma: University of Oklahoma Press, 1963.

Winston, Richard. *Charlemagne.* New York: American Heritage Publishing Company, 1968.

Chronology

742	Birth of Charles
751	Charles's father, Pepin, crowned king of the Franks by order of Pope Zacharias
Sept. 24, 768	Pepin dies
Oct. 9, 768	Charles and his brother, Carloman, elected to rule Frankland as co-regents
769	Charles subdues Aquitaine
771	Carloman dies and Charles becomes sole king of the Franks
772	Charles conducts his first campaign against the Saxons
773	Commences campaign against the Lombards
April 773	Meets Pope Hadrian I in Rome
774	Gains victory in Lombardy, deposing Desiderius and proclaiming himself king
775–76	Campaigns against the Saxons
777	Holds annual council in Paderborn and supervises first mass baptism of Saxons
Aug. 15, 778	Frankish forces en route to Spain ambushed and defeated by Basque guerrillas at Roncesvalles
782	Alcuin arrives in Frankland Charles executes 4,500 Saxons at Verden in reprisal for Frankish defeat by Saxons at Suntel Mountain
785	Negotiates peace with Saxons
788	Annexes Bavaria
791	Adopts palace at Aachen as principal residence
794	Council and General Assembly of Frankfurt
Dec. 25, 800	Charles crowned emperor in Rome by Pope Leo III
806	Publishes *Diviso regni*, a document providing for division of the empire among his three sons after his death
813	Crowns his only surviving son, Louis the Pious, emperor
Feb. 814	Dies, aged 71, of natural causes, at Aachen

Index

Aachen, 38, 57, 61–62, 67, 89, 90
Abd-ar-Rahman, 33
Abul Abbas, 89, 95
"Academy, the," 71
Adalgis, 42–44
Adalperga, 42–43
Alcuin, 67, 68–71, 73
Alps, 26–27
Aquitaine, 17, 22, 99
Arabs, North African, 94
Arichis, duke of Benevento, 42–46
Attila the Hun, 50
Avars, 51, 53–55, 62
Baghdad, 93
    see also Harun al-Rashid
Barcelona, governor of see Suleiman, governor
    of Barcelona
Basques, 34–36
Bavarians, 42, 46–50
Benevento, 42–46
Bertrada (mother of Charles the Great), 16, 22,
    39
Byzantines, 94
Caesar, Julius, 81
caliph of Baghdad see Harun al-Rashid, caliph
    of Baghdad
capitulary, 70
    of 785, 42, 53
    of 797, 53
    see also Charles the Great, domestic
    policy
Carloman (Charles the Great's brother), 18,
    21–22
Carloman, later Pepin (Charles the Great's
    son), 58, 95, 101
Caroline Books, 75
Charlemagne see Charles the Great
Charles (Charles the Great's son), 58, 82–84,
    99, 101
Charles the Bald (Louis the Pious's son), 106
Charles the Great
    children, 22, 23, 25, 35, 58–62, 82–84,
      95, 99, 101
    commissions building programs, 57,
      61–62, 65
    Cordoba, emir of, 31
    cultural tastes, 18, 67, 104–105
    death, 100, 104
    domestic policy, 47, 55, 59–65, 67–76,
      81, 85, 86, 92

early life, 13–18
education, 16, 19
educational policy, 67–71, 73
emperor, 82, 84–87, 89–105
foreign policy, 21–29, 31–39, 41–55, 77,
    82–87, 89, 93–95, 97
king of the Franks, 21–29, 31–39, 41–55,
    57–65, 67–77, 79–82
marriages, 22–24, 28, 39, 50, 82
personal appearance, 21, 32, 79, 92, 95,
    100
personal habits, 31, 55–57, 92
plots against, 43, 50–53
religious beliefs, 13–18, 21, 25, 28–29,
    41, 57, 60, 72–76, 86, 90, 97–99,
    104–105
Roman Catholic church, relations with,
    72–7, 79–80, 83–8, 97–99
Charles Martel ("The Hammer," Charles the
    Great's grandfather), 16, 32, 35
Childeric III, king of Frankland, 15, 17
Christianity, 14–15, 72–77, 90
Churchill, Winston, 8
Clovis I, king of Frankland, 14, 15
Constantine VI, emperor of the Eastern
    Roman Empire, 75
Constantinople, 94
Contasini, Mario, 8
de Tocqueville, Alexis, 9, 11
Decree Concerning the Estates, 64–65
Democracy in America, 9
Desideria (Charles the Great's second wife),
    22, 23, 25
    see also Desiderius; Lombards
Desiderius, king of Lombardy, 22, 23, 25–27,
    42–47
Dürer, Albrecht, 31
Einhard, 85
Emerson, Ralph Waldo, 10, 11
Fastrada (Charles the Great's fourth wife), 23,
    39
Federalist Papers, 10
Frankland, 15, 17, 18, 24, 27, 47–49, 59–61,
    102–107
Franks
    customs, civil, 13, 15, 17, 21, 22, 47,
      82–83
    customs, military, 28, 31, 34, 36, 43, 98
    Roman Catholic church, relations with,
      14–18, 25–28, 72–76, 79–80, 83–86,

97–99
Führerprinzip, 9
Ganelon, 90
Germanic peoples *see* Franks; Lombards; Saxons; Bavarians
Gisla (Charles the Great's sister), 95
Godfred, king of Denmark, 94
Greeks *see* Byzantines
Hadrad, 52
Hadrian I, 26–28, 46, 47, 48, 61, 72–76
Hamilton, Alexander, 10
Harun al-Rashid, caliph of Baghdad, 31–35, 89, 92
heresy, 75
Hildegarde (Charles the Great's third wife), 22, 25, 28, 36, 39, 58
Himiltrude (Charles the Great's first wife), 22, 23, 50, 58
Hitler, Adolf, 8
Holy Land, 90–91, 93
Hrodrud (Charles the Great's daughter), 95
Irminsul, 25
James, William, 8
Karlsburg, 36
Lenin, Vladimir, 8
Leo III, 79, 80, 82–86, 87
Lincoln, Abraham, 11
Liutgard (Charles the Great's fifth wife), 23, 61, 81
Liutperga, 42, 46
Lombards, 17–18, 22, 23, 25–28, 42–47, 82
Lothar (Charles the Great's son), 36
Lothar (Louis the Pious's son), 107
Louis the German, 106
Louis the Pious (Charles the Great's son), 32, 35, 58, 99–100, 103, 106
Marxism, 7, 8
Miami, Florida, 8
Middle East, 90–93
missi dominici, 63, 65
Mongols, 51
Moslems, 16, 31–35, 57, 90–92
    see also Harun al-Rashid, caliph of Baghdad
National Assembly, 47
Niebuhr, Reinhold, 10
Northmen, 94, 96–98, 102, 106
Odo of Metz, 61
Orestes, emperor of Rome, 85
Paderborn, 29, 31, 33, 80, 83

Palace School, 67–71
Pampeluna, 34
    see also Pamplona
Pamplona, 34
Pavia, 26–28
Pepin (formerly Carloman; Charles the Great's son), 58, 95, 101
Pepin the Hunchback (Charles the Great's son), 22, 52, 55, 58
Pepin the Short (king of Frankland; Charles the Great's father), 13–18, 21–22, 45
    Roman Catholic church, relations with, 15–18, 26–28
Pyrenees, 34–36, 38
Roland, 35–37
Roman Empire, Eastern, 93–94
Roman Empire, Western, 15, 18, 48, 79, 89
Rome, 26, 28, 77, 79–86, 93
Roncesvalles, battle of, 34–38, 51
    see also Roland; *Song of Roland*
Roosevelt, Franklin D., 8
St. Heribert's comb, 77
St. James, 59
St. John Lateran, church of, 84
St. Peter, 84
St. Peter's Basilica, 28, 83, 86
Saracens, 16, 31
Saxons, 23–25, 28–29, 33, 36–39, 41–43, 45, 54–55, 93
Sigiburg, Battle of, 28
Slavs, 50–51
Song of Roland, 34–37
Spain, 31–35, 38, 57
Spanish March, 38
Stephen II, 13–17
Suleiman, governor of Barcelona, 31
Suntel Mountain, Battle of, 37–38
Tassilo, duke of Bavaria, 41, 42, 46–49, 52
tithes, 42
Tolstoy, Leo, 7
Tours, Battle of, 16, 33
Venice, 94
Verden, 37–38, 42
Verdun, Peace of, 106
Vikings *see* Northmen
War and Peace, 7
Widukind, 28, 36, 41, 44, 45, 47
Wilson, Woodrow, 8
Zacharias, 15
Zangara, Giuseppe, 8

Susan Banfield writes textbooks and other works for young people, mainly in the areas of history and language. A graduate of Yale College and Teachers College, Columbia University, she has spent several summers in France and has a special love of that country's history and culture. She is also the author of *Charles de Gaulle* and *Joan of Arc* in the Chelsea House series WORLD LEADERS PAST & PRESENT.

Arthur M. Schlesinger, jr., taught history at Harvard for many years and is currently Albert Schweitzer Professor of the Humanities at City University of New York. He is the author of numerous highly praised works in American history and has twice been awarded the Pulitzer Prize. He served in the White House as special assistant to presidents Kennedy and Johnson.